The People's Game:
Football Fandom in Zimbabwe

Manase Kudzai Chiweshe

Langaa Research & Publishing CIG
Mankon, Bamenda

Publisher:

Langaa RPCIG

Langaa Research & Publishing Common Initiative Group
P.O. Box 902 Mankon
Bamenda
North West Region
Cameroon
Langaagrp@gmail.com
www.langaa-rpcig.net

Distributed in and outside N. America by African Books Collective
orders@africanbookscollective.com
www.africanbookscollective.com

ISBN-10: 9956-762-94-6

ISBN-13: 978-9956-762-94-1

© Manase Kudzai Chiweshe 2017

Dedication

To Arnold Enock Chiweshe,
who died before seeing these great things

Table of Contents

Acknowledgements

This book is a culmination of an effort that includes multiple people who have been important in my academic journey. Firstly I thank my mother and my late father for everything that I am today. I also thank my brothers and sisters for all their love and support. My gratitude to Annah Leanne and Munyaradzi Chiweshe, my inspiration and the reason I wake and work everyday. To Tanya, Chido, Vongai, Tafadzwa, Tatenda, Sifelani, Rose and Tia-Mazvi, I love you. And to the love of my life, Faffie Makawa, thank you. I am also forever grateful to all my friends, colleagues and people who have in one way or another mentored and nurtured my academic career. This book is for you all.

Acknowledgements

Chapter I

Introduction and Background

My football journey begins

My earliest memories are littered with football anecdotes which provide fond longing of a childhood in the poor flats of Mbare, Harare. I am a second generation football fan, raised on a steady stable diet of Zimbabwean football. My childhood was largely under the influence of Rufaro Stadium in Mbare. I grew up with a father who loved football, a lifelong Dynamos fan who socialised his children into a deep rooted relationship with the local team. Growing up, my father would take us to games together with two of my brothers. I remember fondly those days because they mean so much now that he has passed away. My father was a quite man normally but I have vivid memories of his animation when he narrated of past heroes he saw such as Archiford Chimutanda, the man who he claims never trained but still found a way to make defenders look stupid or Oliver Kateya, Joel Shambo and the eternal George Shaya.

These were names I grew up with, fascinated by the game and how it meant so much to its fans. I am a fifth born child in a family of seven. I mainly grew up with my brothers: one older and one younger than me. It is this history that shapes the long football journey which forms the background to this book. This book traces the important patterns in Zimbabwean football fandom. It demonstrates the nexus between social identity and supporting a sports team. The book highlights that there are deeper underlying meanings and assumptions to one's support of a sporting team. From the intense regional rivalry that characterized medieval ball games to the national, religious, ethnic and political antagonisms that are present in modern day football, one can highlight the continued role of football in the processes of identity construction and maintenance. I explore how fan identities are formed and how they mediate in fans' social lives. Supporting a football team is more than just going to the stadium; rather it transcends one's social being. Being a fan becomes an important part of one's social identity and affects most aspects of one's life. There is something more to supporting a football team besides entertainment.

Why football fandom?

Sport plays a vital role in modern contemporary society. Its prominence in the media, which devotes considerably more coverage to sport than politics or economics, demonstrates its expansion during the last century (Keim 2003). This phenomenon has had different impacts on the development of nations, cultures and communities. Sport forms an integral part of life for the majority of people, whether as active participants or spectators. The importance of sport as a pacifying force is thus well documented. Sport is also regarded as a possible tool of social interaction because it occasions collective experiences, as well as direct physical contact, between the participants.

According to Harms, people jointly participating in active sport, especially in team sports, enter into "direct physical contact" with one another, which practically provokes "the emergence of intensive interpersonal relationships" (Harms 1982: 7). Wann et al (2001) argues from a structural functionalist perspective that spectator sports have an institutional structure that affords fans to experience a range of euphoric and dysphoric emotions. This provides affective payoffs that help combat the pernicious effects of apathy and cessation of motivation, a condition that can prove fatal to any social system. The survival of a social system thus depends not only on living and working, struggling and persevering, but also joking, laughing, cheering and celebrating.

This book provides an alternative way to understanding communities and how sport can be viewed as a serious lens into societal organisations. It offers important insights into how Africans are also engaged in leisure activities and that play is also part of our life worlds. Given the major focus on poverty, disease and conflict, African stories of intimate play and enjoyment tend to be marginalised. Soccer has the power to bring together or divide communities. In Africa, everyday ethnic and religious rivalries are played out through football matches. It is thus important to capture this space and use football as a way to heal historical and deep-seated conflicts. As Alegi (2010) points out, from its colonial origins, football served as a nation-building instrument from decolonization to independence.

National teams remain an important means for expressing national identities. However, beyond national identities or nation building, football has rooted itself in African culture. Alegi (2010) argues that by 1960, football was an established component of African urban culture. National football teams in Africa have historically been used as tools to foster national identity with varying success across the continent overtime. In football there always exists another game. The match consists of more than the players' tactical skills; the coach's training methods or the final results of the match. It goes beyond the gates of the stadium to influence everyday life. "Football matches are explained and represented in many different ways: as an allegory of life and emotions; as a drama of success and decline; as an inexplicable mystery; or as a match. Whether dusty playing fields, provincial stadiums, or high-tech 'sports domes', football pitches offer arenas not only for the match, but also for the production of public spheres and imaginary spaces where social, cultural and political praxis and discourses are created, celebrated and negotiated" Baller 2006: 326) Football is thus played both on the pitch and beyond.

Football is a charged political and ideological structure where power and identity battles are fought both on the surface and through subtexts (Pannenborg 2010). Researching sport is not, and should not be restricted to sport but should be seen to open up wider avenues of enquiry into everyday life. Burdsey and Chappell (2002) in a study on social identity and football in Scotland and Northern Ireland try to show the nexus between social identity and football. Drawing on theories of social identity, they highlight the manner in which supporting particular football clubs in these nations operates alongside other social processes to constitute individuals' social identities.

They argue that one's affiliation with a particular club represents the combination of a number of specific social, political and religious attributes and that football remains one of the few public arenas in which the exhibition and articulation of these sentiments is permitted. MacClancy (1996: 2) states that "sport in general and football in particular are vehicles of identity, providing people with a sense of difference and a way of classifying themselves and others, whether latitudinally or hierarchically". More specifically, they argue that ultimately a football match offers an expressive support for the affirmation of collective identity and local, regional and national antagonisms. Supporting a particular football team, not only facilitates a feeling of shared identity with fellow supporters, it also acts as a means of differentiating oneself from other groups.

By 1960, football was an established component of African urban culture in Zimbabwe. Africans have learned, adopted, and achieved a noticeable cultural appropriation of the game across the continent. Giullianotti (2004) offers an illuminating account of Zimbabwean football showing its historical development from colonial period. The Pioneer Column's men were the first players of football and rugby (Thompson 1935 in Giullianotti (2004)). Several sports clubs had been set up by 1900 in the emerging towns catering for competition in football and other sports. Organised sport was the sole privilege of whites. Football was particularly popular amongst new arrivals from Britain but Rhodesian schools educated boys in cricket and rugby.

Football was probably introduced to blacks from 1923 by black miner workers from Transvaal migrated north to arrive in Bulawayo and Midlands to look for work and playing football in their spare time. Local Africans thus favored football because it required little economic and cultural capital compared to other sports. Township clubs sprung up through the 1920s and 1930s, one of the oldest and most successful being the Lions Club of Bulawayo (renamed Matabeleland Highlanders in 1937) which was formed by the grand children of the last Ndebele king, Lobengula. Football was avenue for expressions of ethnic pride and intercultural rivalry, notably between Ndebele and Shona peoples within clubs (Giullianotti 2004).

The importance of football in the everyday lives of its fans cannot be overemphasized. Porat (2010: 277) using examples from Israel conclude "that supporting a football club is a life-long project that begins at an early age and ends with the life of the fan. Such studies unequivocally indicate that football fandom is a way of life. The fan's daily and weekly agenda is determined by his/her relationship with the football club. Most importantly, football fandom is a significant component of identity: it is stable and effective." Chiweshe (2016) using the example of Dynamos Football Club fans in Zimbabwe demonstrate the nexus between social identity and supporting a football club. He concludes that "There is something more to supporting a football team besides entertainment. Supporting a football team is a kind of marriage, a commitment similar to 'till death do us part'" (Chiweshe 2016: 101). Bill Murray (1994) acknowledges that the practice of soccer is a cultural form in Africa, the most important of which is the nature and practice soccer fandom. He argues that soccer has always been regarded as the game of the people and attracts their participation, which ranges from moderate involvement to committed and animated identification.

With the growing complexity and fragmentation of the modern and postmodern society sociologists have postulated that the social worlds and opportunities for collective identity in sport raise it to a higher level of social importance. Indeed Dunning (1988) suggested that identification with a sports team can provide people with an important identity prop, a source of "we-feeling" and a sense of belonging in what would otherwise be an isolated existence. It seems reasonable to suggest, therefore, that fandom comprises more than simply attending and observing a sporting event. Rather, being a fan represents an association from which the individual derives considerable emotional and value significance. This acknowledgement that sports fandom consists of more than overt behavior has important implications for the choice of research methodology. Supporting a particular football team not only facilitates a feeling of shared identity with fellow supporters, it also acts as a means of differentiating oneself from other groups (Jenkins, 1996).

In many cases identification with a particular team indicates what or who one is, and equally importantly, what or who they are not. Hughson and Free (2006) illustrate how through two fans of Wolverhampton Wanderers in England engage in symbolic activities as making a bedroom a private temple to the team. The fans humanise, decorate and invest with meanings their common life spaces and social practices. Paraphernalia such as scarves, flags, and team posters are infused with meaning in a particular cultural context in which financial, emotional, and symbolic investments are experienced as collectively meaningful cultural form. Fans are thus continuously involved individual and collective interpretive engagement with the game in process. Football fandom is premised on the construction of shared identities between fans that define and differentiate themselves from rivals.

Methodological framework

This book is based on multiple fieldwork processes with fans in Zimbabwe spanning a period of eight years including desk research, interviews, observation, focus group discussions and netnography. This section provides the methodology used across the chapters in the book. The overall research paradigm is based on qualitative research methodology that sought to provide a voice of the fans on the notions of identity and attachments. Qualitative methodologies are strong in that the use of interviews and observations provides a deep, rather than broad, set of knowledge about a particular phenomenon, and they are appropriate to investigate cognitive and affective aspects of fandom. They allow for a better understanding of psychological factors such as affect and cognition, which are important in sports fandom (Jones 1994).

They help understand the deeper meaning and reasons why fans support a sporting team. Qualitative methodologies allow the cognitive and affective components of fandom to be explored in greater depth than quantitative methodologies. They encourage the informant to introduce concepts of importance from the emic aspect, rather than adhering to subject areas that have been pre-determined by the researcher. Fandom is a difficult aspect to quantify and it is only through stories of a respondent's lives that you begin to realize how supporting sporting team is uniquely intertwined with their existence and definition of themselves.

Using qualitative methods thus allowed for a nuanced understanding of how fans define themselves. Through interviews, life stories and focus group discussions one can easily follow the stories and gain richer understanding of the underlying issues in fandom and social identity. They allow for a better understanding of psychological factors such as affect and cognition which are important in sports fandom. Qualitative methods also permit the identification of longitudinal changes in fandom, whereas quantitative approaches tend to take a "snapshot" of behavior, cognition or affect at the one time the research is conducted (Jones 1994). The chapters are based on the methodological steps outlined in Table 1.1 below.

Table 1.1: Methodological approach

Chapter	Methodology	Journal or Book Published
1	Desk research is the analysis of information that already exists, in one form or another. This information was easily available since it had been already collected over the years for purposes other than that of this project. This secondary research technique involves a literature review or analysis. The researcher is involved in mining already existing data: "pull out" relevant data or information; summarize it; logically analyze and/or statistically treat it; and report results. Material used included newspapers, articles, journals, books, magazines and on line reports on football in Zimbabwe.	Unpublished

| 2 | The study concentrated on the use of a mainly qualitative methodology. The research used an approach that sought to hear from the fans themselves on the notions of identity and attachments to the team. Qualitative methodologies are strong in that the use of open-ended interviews, focused group discussions and observations provide a deep, rather than broad, set of knowledge about a particular phenomenon. Such methodologies are appropriate to investigate cognitive and affective aspects of fandom. They allow for a better understanding of psychological factors, such as affect and cognition, which are important in sports | Chiweshe, Manase Kudzai (2011) 'Understanding the processes of becoming a football team fan in an African context: the case of Dynamos Football Club fans in Zimbabwe', *Soccer & Society*, 12: 2, 174 — 183 |

	fandom. They help one understand the deeper meaning and reasons of why fans support a sporting team.	
3	A total of eight focus group discussions and thirty in depth interviews were conducted with fans which were sampled through purposive sampling. Each group discussion had an average of 11 respondents. Purposive sampling technique was used to target fans at stadiums and training sessions. The research tended to follow the most exuberant fans dressed in team colours and fancy clothing on match days. These fans usually sing with drums throughout the matches thus provided an initial entry into getting access to other fans. The focus group discussions and	Chiweshe Manase Kudzai (2016): Till death do us part: football as part of everyday life amongst Dynamos Football Club fans in Zimbabwe, *African Identities*, DOI: 10.1080/14725843.2015.1102703

	interviews were conducted at a variety of places which included homes of fans, community centres and Raylton Sports Club where the team held training sessions. Respondents were drawn from suburbs in Harare such as Mufakose, Waterfalls, Chitungwiza, Highfield, Mbare, Sunningdale and Mt Pleasant. In total, hundred-twenty fans were covered by the study the majority being male (hundred) which shows the gendered dimensions of fandom.	
4	This chapter is based on extensive review of literature. It utilised a desk research approach that focused on collecting data from journals, books, monographs, newspapers, magazines,	Unpublished

	on line sources and reports. Such an approach allowed for a nuanced understanding of the various dimensions of football rivalries in Zimbabwe.	
5	The study utilised in-depth interviews and focus group discussions to ensure that voices of female fans are properly documented and outlined. As an exploratory study into female fan identities in Zimbabwe, the study sought a small sample to allow for in-depth investigation. A sample of thirty women was selected from women attending games at Rufaro Stadium in Harare. They were chosen from six different teams over a period of three weeks to ensure a level of representativeness of teams in the league. Two focus group	Chiweshe, M.K. 2014. One of the boys: female fans" responses to the masculine and phallocentric nature of football stadiums in Zimbabwe, *Critical African Studies*, DOI: 10.1080/21681392.2014.940077

	discussions with five participants each were conducted. The whole study thus focused on the lived experiences of forty female fans that ranged between 22 and 43 years of age.	
6	Observation allowed for an understanding of fan overt fan behaviors. Observation was limited to mainly Harare (ten matches) and Bulawayo (one match) due to the cost involved in travelling to various parts of the country. The league in Zimbabwe however is dominated by teams in Harare (at one time 8 out of 16 teams are based in the capital). Other matches observed were for the national team (two) and training sessions of teams such as Dynamos. The stadium turned to be an important source of	Unpublished

	information on fan identities. Before games and during games it was easy to initiate discussions around supporting football and how people came to love the teams they support.	
7	The study conducted a total of eight focused group discussions and thirty in-depth interviews with Dynamos fans selected through purposive sampling technique. For comparative purposes between generations of fans the study separated into two groups: Group 1 (those who are forty years and above) and Group 2 (those below forty years). The majority of informants were male which highlights male dominated nature of football fandom in Zimbabwe.	Unpublished

	Observation was conducted during eight games in which the team played against various opposition played in Harare. During such matches I was involved in informal discussions with fans.	
8	Interviews with forty fans were conducted in Harare. The fans were selected using a snowballing technique and targeting of fans attending football matches and club training sessions. This sampling technique was necessitated by the lack of an updated fan register. To complement the interviews, the study utilised observation of fan behaviors during two national team games in Harare. This informal observation was based on the need to understand how fans	Chiweshe, M.K. 2013. Online Football Fan Identities and Cyber-fandoms in Zimbabwe, In *Identity and Nation in African Football: Fans, Community and Clubs*, Chuka Onwumechili and Gerard Akindes (Eds), New York: Palgrave Macmillan

	of rival clubs relate in the context of the stadium. The study also utilised netnography to understand online football communities in Zimbabwe. Kozinets (2002: 61) notes that netnography "is ethnography adapted to the study of online communities. As a method, "netnography" is better suited for understanding on line communications than traditional ethnography, and is more naturalistic and unobtrusive than focus groups or interviews. It provides information on the symbolism, meanings, and consumption patterns of online consumer groups."	

Football fandoms in Zimbabwe

The outward expression of fandom manifests itself in various ways among football fans in Zimbabwe. Different sets of supporters have differing ways of celebrating loyalty to their teams. Fans of the now defunct Motor Action, which was bankrolled by businessman Eric Rosen and his wife, had a band. This band had instruments such as drums, pipes, and trumpets. The team owned the instruments, and was known as the Mighty Bulls and the fans dressed in team colors with red flags that had bullhorns on them. Motor Action was formed from the defunct club, Blackpool. At one time, Blackpool reached the semi-final of a continental competition and lost the league to Dynamos under controversial circumstances. The success of that team, popularly named *Ndochi*, ensured Motor Action inherited sizeable number of fans.

Flags are important markers of fan identity. The flags contain important symbols or team badges. Highlanders' fans sport black and white flags with a shield with a spear and stick with the words *Siyinqaba* (We are a fortress) underneath. Fans indicate that the team badge illustrates the warrior-like nature of the team. Highlanders (nicknamed *Bosso*) are thus a fortress, an army and a haven for its supporters in general and Ndebele people in particular. Fans from Highlanders all agreed that the black and white colors worn by their team are a celebration of the club's African heritage. As the oldest black club in Zimbabwe, they claim to be the first peoples' team.

Colors are important for fans because they represent team identity and, thus, difference from opponents. Fans in most cases ensure they wear the same colors as their teams. There are many cases of fans being abused at the stadium for wearing the wrong colors. Caps United fans take everything with the green color to be a symbol of their team. For instance, fans of this team are known for coming to games with tree leaves, cabbages or green vegetables as a way of celebrating their team. Opposition fans have often accused Caps of causing deforestation whenever they play. Others have chided them by calling the team *mufushwa* (sun-dried vegetables). For Dynamos' fans, the color blue is a symbol of heaven's approval for their team. The fans all retort, 'If God hated Dynamos, He would not have made the sky blue.'

A fan from Motor Action noted that his team wears red because it is associated with champions such as Arsenal, Liverpool, and Manchester United. The color red is, thus, intimidating to opponents. Gunners, another defunct team was formed originally by Arsenal fans, also wears red. Expression of fan identities also takes place through song and dance. Chiweshe (2010) argues that songs are an integral part of stadium culture and express love for the team and hatred for rivals. Collinson (2009: 16) adds that songs are indispensable to football fans because, aside from their own massed physical presence, bedecked in team colors and the deploying flags and banners, they have little control over the visual appearance of a stadium.

Football songs are a form of language that conveys meaning not only about the game but about a society's culture in general. Fans use songs to motivate their players by praising their masculinity as a way of increasing their performance levels. Many such songs portray the maleness and virility of the team; for example Dynamos fans sing '*DeMbare yaita mamonya*' (Dynamos have strong men). The feeling is that a real fan comes to the stadium to be part of the singing and not just to watch the game. To affirm your fan credentials, one has to engage in the singing. Songs are an integral part of stadium culture however; the nature of songs and how they influence or are influenced by dominant ideas in society needs to be understood.

Structure of the book

The book has nine themed chapters focusing on various aspects of football fandom in Zimbabwe. Chapter 2 provides the context of understanding how one becomes a fan. It uses a case study of Dynamos Football Club to highlight how the process of socialisation into a fan happens. It highlights that the process of becoming a fan is context specific and highly individualised.Chapter 3 demonstrates the nexus between social identity and supporting a football club. It draws on concepts of social identity to show how supporting a football club operates to constitute an important part of individuals' social identities. The chapter explores the importance of supporting a football team in the everyday lives of fans.

Chapter 4 provides an analysis of how football can be used to cement, reproduce and celebrate historical conflicts. The chapter questions the simplistic assumptions of a growing field of sports for development which sees football as a vehicle for social development. Using football rivalries in Zimbabwe as an example, the chapter highlights how sport can be a vehicle of playing out conflicts and passing rivalries from one generation to the next. The chapter explores the intertwined historical, political, ethno-regional among other causes of rivalries reflecting how football reproduces underlying fractures that exist in society.

In Chapter 5, I outline the experiences of female fans who attend matches in Zimbabwe. The chapter provides a nuanced analysis of female fans' responses to the masculine and phallocentric nature of the football stadium. In Zimbabwe women fans are increasing in number, challenging the dominant belief that stadiums are no-go areas for women. Using in-depth interviews and focus group discussions with forty female fans, the chapter highlights how women react, negotiate and respond to misogynistic and vulgar songs and chants. Chapter 6 focuses on the creation and recreation of women's bodies through songs and chants among football fans that are misogynistic in nature. It offers an analysis of how stadiums are arenas for the celebration and reinforcement of hegemonic masculinities.

Football fandom has proved a fertile ground for the display of masculine identities and the stadium has proved a readymade arena for the playing out of these identities. Chapter 7 provides an analysis of the creation of symbols associated with teams such as nicknames, colours and rituals. The chapter uses Dynamos Football Club as an example. Chapter 8 uses netnography to explore presentation and contestation of fan identities on Facebook. The chapter outlines actual conditions, motivation, symbolic meaning, and performance of online fan identities. The virtual nature of these fan identities is part of entrenched nature of our increasingly bifurcated society.

Chapter II

Understanding the Processes of Becoming a Football Team Fan in an African Context: The Case of Dynamos Football Club Fans in Zimbabwe

Introduction

From the intense regional rivalry that characterized medieval ball games to the national, religious, ethnic and political antagonisms that are present in modern-day football, one can highlight the continued role of football in the processes of identity construction and maintenance. Football/soccer is the most popular sport in the African continent and a source of entertainment for millions of people. Whilst the popularity of soccer in the continent is a question to be answered elsewhere in terms of globalization and colonization, this chapter seeks to analyse the process of becoming a fan of a particular team in the continent (Darby 2000).

This research can be used as a basis to understand why some teams are more supported and why, in some instances, new clubs have failed to attract fans. Being a fan is a historical process in which one makes a commitment to a particular team. A gap exists in the prevalent literature on identity formation with regard to sports fandom in an African context. The current sociology of sport literature does not adequately address the creation of fan identity, especially within non-Western contexts. Social science research on sport fans focuses largely on the effects of fandom, for example, the violence and aggression, which may result from being a fan. Little is known, however, about the process of becoming a fan, especially in a Zimbabwean context. Becoming a fan of a particular team is context specific and differs from one person to the other.

Brief background of Dynamos Football Club

The history of Dynamos is a contested terrain. There are various versions of its formation which are contradictory, but this chapter offers a brief look at some of the stories. Dynamos Football Club was formed in 1963 in Salisbury, now Harare. Northern Rhodesia at that time was under Roy Welensky and African nationalism was on the rise. There was segregation according to race in all walks of life, including football. Blacks were relegated to the zonal township SADAFA amateur league, while the whites played in their own organized league. However, some radical whites saw the benefits of mixing in soccer since it would improve the quality of the sport. Thus, in 1961, a multiracial league was formed which had two black teams from Salisbury, namely Salisbury City and United. The league, however, collapsed at the end of 1962 due to financial constraints (Mutungamiri 1998).

The players from the two black Salisbury teams were left in the cold but they continued to meet and train at the Number 5 Grounds in Harare Township (now Mbare, National). This was made easier since most of them worked together at Tobacco Sales Floor in the industrial site near Harare Township. These players then organized a match against Salisbury Yellow Peril, a team which was the best in the Salisbury Amateur League. The group could not play without an identity; thus one of the players, a certain Nercasio Murambiwa, having heard of Dinamo Kiev in Russia, suggested the name Dynamos. Sam Dauya who was the club's first secretary then liaised with Ken Walker who was Operations Manager at the Sales Floor, and the name was endorsed in consultation with other players.

Dauya claimed that Walker goes down as the founder of the club, as shown by the first letterhead that was used by Dynamos, something that one of the first players interviewed disagrees with, claiming that Walker only played a peripheral role and it was the players that founded the club. The first match at Gwanzura Stadium was well supported and Dynamos beat Yellow Peril. The massive support that followed this match left the authorities feeling threatened, and according to Dauya, at one time, they took steps to ban the club thinking that it may soon become a front for a political party. Dauya claimed that he was harassed at odd hours by security agents of the colonial government. In years to come, Dynamos would become the most celebrated and successful club, and only nine years after its formation an article in one of the most popular newspapers of Zimbabwe described Dynamos as the glamour club of Rhodesia (Mutungamiri 1998).

Understanding fandom: an international perspective

There has been a considerable amount of research on the process of becoming football fans, especially in Europe (Burdsey and Chappel 2002; Giulianotti and Robertson 2006) and in North and South America. In Brazil and Argentina, soccer offers a display of in-group and out-group identities (Giulianotti 1999). Inclusion and exclusion from supporting clubs mainly works on the basis of race, sex and geographical location. Fans tend to support clubs from their home areas. In most cases, fans tend to over-identify with their clubs and may view clubs as an extension of the self and invest too much emotionally in their clubs. This can produce negative effects, including depressive behaviour or even violence. Sir Norman Chester for Football Research Centre at the University of Leicester offers a broad understanding into the process of becoming a fan within the English context.

Football clubs offer a collective and symbolic focus for a sense of belonging and pride in a local community. Football clubs have even been described as a nonreligious form of devotion. Perhaps it is no coincidence that some players are called 'god' by fans. The Liverpool author, Alan Edge, calls his book on following Liverpool FC *Faith in our Fathers*, and has chapter headings which imitate religious practices. The Centre analysed the '1991 When Saturday Comes study' carried out by a magazine and the results highlight a number of factors influencing supporting a particular club. The first is the influence of a male relative, especially a father who takes his children to games from a young age. Other factors included local pride, family influence, peers, success/cup runs, team colours, style of play and club initiative (Sir Norman Chester Centre For Football Research 2002).

Drawing on theories of social identity in Scotland and Ireland, the manner in which supporting particular football clubs in these nations operates alongside other social processes to constitute individuals' social identities has been highlighted. One's affiliation with a particular club represents the combination of a number of specific social, political and religious attributes and football remains one of the few public arenas in which the exhibition and articulation of these sentiments are permitted (Burdsey and Chappel 2002). It can thus be concluded that 'sport in general and football in particular are vehicles of identity, providing people with a sense of difference and a way of classifying themselves and others, whether latitudinally or hierarchically' (MacClancy 1996: 2).

Defining a fan in the context of present research

The distinction between a fan and a spectator is vital in any worthy attempt to methodologically explain what or who can be termed a Dynamos fan. Whereas a spectator of sport will observe a spectacle and forgets it very quickly, the fan continues his interest until the intensity of feelings towards the team becomes so great that parts of everyday are devoted to the team (Duke 1991). Thus, for the purpose of this research, a Dynamos fan is one whose interest in the team goes beyond simply watching games but affects other parts of his life. A Dynamos fan is one who sees the team as an extension of themselves such that when they talk about the team, they talk as if they are talking of themselves. In simple terms, it is someone who attends matches, knows the history and symbols of the team, has fond memories of past matches, and remembers the first match they attended and talks passionately about the team.

Process of becoming a fan among Dynamos Football Club fans

Results from the two research groups (40 years and above and less than 40) highlight a number of stories about how one becomes a Dynamos Football Club fan. The results from the two groups are presented separately below:

Group one (40 years and above)

The 15 respondents in this group gave a very diverse range of reasons for supporting Dynamos. One respondent claimed that he fell in love with the style of play from the first game in 1963 that they played against a team called Yellow Peril. Another respondent said that he became a fan after watching Daniel 'Dhidhidhi' Ncube scoring six goals as Dynamos beat Sakubva 8–1 in 1973. Personal ties with players was another reason for supporting the team as most of the players stayed in one of the most populous black townships (Harare Township now Mbare). One of the respondents indicated that he became a fan to support Dauya (founder) who lived a couple of houses from him in Mbirimi Drive. Another respondent claimed that he was attracted by the multi-ethnic composition of the team.

It accommodated players from many ethnic groups at a time when the colonial regime used tactics of dividing people according to ethnicity. Among the players, the respondents highlighted people such as Josiah Akende of Malawian origin and Sarupinda who were Manyika. The ethnic origin of certain players was also an important draw card for fans from those ethnic groups. The two focus group discussions held for this group also brought out a number of divergent views. In the focus group discussions, the respondents mainly focused on the state of football in colonial Rhodesia, which was mainly racist. At that time, teams were mainly owned by whites and although blacks played for these teams they suffered racial abuse. One of the respondents personally knew one of the first Dynamos players Danny Bricks who had played for Salisbury Callies and had left because of racism.

Respondents noted that what was most attractive about Dynamos was that it was wholly black from the administration to the players. It formed the face of resistance against racial apartheid not only within football, but also in the wider society. This might explain why Dauya was harassed by security agents, who were afraid that it was a front for a political party. The founder member who was interviewed, noted that although Dynamos did not align with any political party, officially the players also wanted independence like other blacks in the country. The colonial government was afraid of the influence such a popular organization with the masses would cause. They were afraid that its interests were more than soccer but they might have been unable to ban it fearing the reaction of the masses. Forming political parties was dangerous at that time but soccer teams were allowed, which in a way highlights the agency of blacks who were denied the right of political association, but with soccer they could meet in crowds freely.

A respondent in the focus group discussions said that he became a fan of Dynamos because it represented a fight against segregation and racism. However, he claimed that the link between Dynamos and Zimbabwe African National Unity (This was the political wing of one of the armed groups fighting for the liberation of Zimbabwe. At independence in 1980 under Robert Mugabe it became the first black led government of Zimbabwe) was purely coincidental for him. The fact that they were both formed in 1963 does not mean they shared the same goals, ambitions and views. Another respondent claimed that although it is difficult to ignore the political situation of the 1960s, he mainly became a fan for footballing reasons; the team was entertaining and had some of the best talent in the country. For another fan, the only political issue he could link to him becoming a fan was that Dynamos offered him an escape from the stress and humiliation he suffered from his brutal white employers.

Within the focus group discussions, one respondent claimed that football matches offered a place where people could freely mingle without much harassment from the brutal police force. He said that in the huge crowds that Dynamos games attracted people talked about many issues, including politics. He further alluded to the notion that some people, who were involved in nationalistic politics at that time, used football stadiums and crowds as a cover for their meetings and discussions. Another old respondent claimed that the colonial government was mostly afraid of the organization of Dynamos and how it had mobilized support within the townships.

Group two (below 40 years)

The findings for the unstructured in-depth interviews of the first objective for group two (those aged below 40 years) highlighted that 10 of the 15 respondents in the sample were primarily influenced to support Dynamos by a male relative, especially their fathers. For all the respondents, the first game of football they ever watched was a game that involved Dynamos, and it was in the company of a male relative. In the two focus group discussions, the general finding was that fathers, brothers and peers were very much influential in turning respondents into Dynamos supporters. In the focus group discussions, there was general agreement that fathers tended to impose too much pressure on their sons to support the team and the respondents that had sons also confessed putting similar pressure on them. The fathers of most respondents tended to be influential in turning their children into Dynamos fans. Three of the ten respondents claimed that they were obligated by their fathers to support Dynamos.

One actually claimed that his father made him promise to support the team on his deathbed. The influence of male relatives went to such an extent that all seven respondents claimed that while growing up they had never known about any other team. None of the respondents was influenced by a female relative although four claimed that their mothers supported Dynamos and they used to go to watch the games with their fathers. Six of the respondents attributed the reason for supporting Dynamos to the pressure of their peers and friends. Of these six, three grew up in Mbare where Dynamos originated and played their home games. The other three claimed that almost all the people in their streets they lived supported the team.

One of the respondents who grew up living in Matererini flats, which are near Rufaro Stadium (This is the home ground for Dynamos Football Club located in Mbare suburb in the capital city Harare), acclaims that the only entertainment he had during his growing up were Dynamos home games. He claimed that on such Sundays as a young person he would play around the stadium watching over people's cars for a small fee and would watch the last minutes of the game when the gates were opened for free. The people that surrounded them, such as neighbours and friends, all supported Dynamos. These respondents were thus socialized into supporting Dynamos at an early age to an extent that they are socializing their own children to support the team.

It was interesting to note the difference between the respondents who grew up in Mbare and the other three (two grew in rural areas and the other in Avondale a low-density suburb in Harare) on what the team meant to them. The respondents from Mbare tended to view the team as their own, noting the notion that it came from Mbare and thus it belonged to the people of Mbare. The respondents who grew up in Mbare thus tended to be more zealous and passionate about the team than the others. However, in the focus group discussions, respondents noted that Dynamos has grown beyond being just a Mbare team to one that is fighting for international recognition. Respondents also claimed that although Dynamos has its roots in Mbare, it did not belong to Mbare but to whoever has love and passion for the team at heart. It could also be noted within the focus groups that the team tended to mean different things to different people depending on their background and where they grew up.

All 15 respondents attributed the influence of the media in their decision to support Dynamos. The focus group discussions validated the influence of the media in choosing to support the team. There was general consensus that Dynamos' games dominated football commentaries on radio and most respondents grew up listening to the voices of commentators such as Evans Mambara and Charles Mabika. The main medium for football is live commentaries on radio, which have been provided by the national broadcaster since before independence. The print media has also covered football matches extensively. Television coverage of league matches in Zimbabwe is a recent phenomenon, which is still riddled with problems since the screening of games is not guaranteed.

The respondents in the sample claim that live radio commentaries were influential in turning them into supporters. Great Dynamos sides of the past dominated the soccer scene in Zimbabwe and most of their games were broadcast live on radio. The respondents grew up being familiar with great Dynamos players such as Moses Chunga, Francis Shonhayi and Memory Muchirahowa. The respondents heard so much about Dynamos while growing up that they had an urgency to support the team. Coupled with other factors, such as peer pressure and pressure from fathers, they became fans. To the five respondents, who grew up in the rural areas, the media offered the only source of knowledge about Dynamos. Three of the respondents claim that their fathers had small transistor radios, and they listened to football commentaries on these. The relationship with Dynamos for some of the respondents thus started even before seeing the team play. It was only when they came to Harare that they fulfilled their desire to watch their childhood team play.

Besides the influence of peers, male relatives and media, Dynamos' own success drew a lot of supporters to itself. Most of the respondents, especially those who grew up in rural areas, were attracted by the success the team enjoyed especially in the 1980s and 1990s. Dynamos are the record league champions and have won most of the cups played in Zimbabwe. They were the first and only Zimbabwean club to reach the finals of the African Champions League in 1998, which made it the second team in Southern Africa after South Africa's Orlando Pirates.

Most of the respondents in Group 2 were old enough to understand such achievements, and thus Dynamos' relative success drew them to the club. It was not only the success they were enjoying, but the history of success they had, which also influenced the respondents to support them. All 15 respondents claimed that they were drawn to the club by its history, which includes how it was formed and its former players. Focus group discussions also confirm that the success and history of the team drew respondents within group two to the club. Respondents within the focus group discussions alluded to the notion that they had wanted to be associated with the team of Zimbabwean football legends such as George Shaya, Freddy Mkwesha, Oliver Kateya and Edward Katsvere.

Explaining the process of becoming a fan – a sociological analysis

Becoming a fan is a complex process that is often difficult to explain. Below is a theoretical analysis of the process of becoming a fan as highlighted by the cases noted earlier in this chapter. The cases highlight distinct experiences which can be explained by sociological theory as outlined below.

Socialization into a fan

The influence of family, especially male relatives, has been shown to be very influential in turning one into a fan. The majority of Group 2 respondents argued that they were mainly influenced by their fathers and other male relatives into supporting Dynamos. None was influenced by a female relative, which reinforces the notion of male dominance in soccer. It may explain why all the respondents were male in that fathers rarely take their girl children to the stadiums. Socialization is the process by which we learn to become members of society that has two facets – primary and secondary socialization. It is primary socialization that is most important in turning one into a fan because it is mostly imposed since children do not know many alternatives (Berger 1986).

Children are born with an instinctive capacity for self-development and this is matured in interactions in primary groups such as the family (Cooley 1986). Thus it is within the family as the most important primary group that children learn the basics of fan following. In families where fathers are fans of sporting teams, the children are exposed to sport fanaticism at an early age. The father takes his children to games, buys them club regalia and constantly tells them about the club's success and history. Children as they selfdevelop in interaction within their families become fans of their father's teams.

Basking in reflected glory

Fandom can be created by the desire to be a part of the environment created by a winning team – 'jumping on the bandwagon'. Social identity theory has two processes pertaining to one becoming a fan known as BIRGing (basking in reflected glory) and CORFing (cutting off reflective failures). This can explain why fans decide to support some sporting teams because of their success. BIRGing can be defined as the tendency of individuals to publicize their connection with successful others, when they have not contributed to the other's success. It can thus explain why some fans might overly identify with hugely successful sporting teams. CORFing can be defined as the tendency of individuals to cut off association with failing teams. However, this aspect of the theory is debatable because most failing sporting teams have fans associated with them (Uhler and Murrell 1999).

BIRGing can be used to explain fans who started supporting the team due to its success. The other process of CORFing was proved wrong because respondents showed that they would continue supporting the team even if it failed. Respondents claimed that they would never stop supporting the club under any circumstances. The process of CORFing was thus not supported by the findings of the research, while the process of BIRGing was confirmed by a number of respondents, mostly from Group 2 (aged below 40 years). The process of BIRGing highlights the need for individuals to associate with individuals or institutions that are more successful than them. These individuals then become so attached to such institutions that the success and failure of these institutions is felt at a personal level.

Structure–agency dichotomy

Structuration theory allows for an understanding of the political conditions that existed at the formation of Dynamos. This approach also allows fans to be viewed as capable actors who act rationally and respond to the dictates of structures. Structuration theory, which gives the structure the same value as it gives to agency and appreciates the dialectic and complimentary relationship that exists between the two (Giddens 1984), allowed the researcher to understand how most respondents in the colonial era turned into Dynamos fans. Within most societies, there are a variety of means by which social identity can be expressed; yet for many (particularly minority) groups, football can be the sole or, at least the primary, outlet for such sentiments (Duke 1991).

In colonial Rhodesia, rights of the blacks were disregarded by the whites and they could not freely associate because repressive laws made it dangerous for blacks to organize themselves politically. The structures (colonial government) were thus constraining blacks, yet as active agents, they realized the potential of organizing football teams and using such teams as a celebration of their identity as blacks. The founder member and former player of Dynamos, interviewed in this research, confirmed the notion that playing for Dynamos at that time was like playing for all the black masses. Respondents thus said that they supported the team because it was wholly black and represented a face of resistance to the brutal colonizers. This explanation is valid for respondents in Group 1, who were converted into Dynamos fans during the colonial period.

Conclusion

This chapter has outlined the process of becoming a fan in an African context noting the experiences of two different generations of supporters. It has also attempted to understand the complexities and various factors involved in the process of becoming a fan. The chapter offers a sociological analysis into some of the processes involved, thereby showing how the socialization process remains one of the most important factors in determining the team one ends up supporting. Whilst studies of football fandom have proved a popular source of enquiry within the sociology of sport, as this chapter has shown, there is still a great deal of research that can be done in this area, especially in Africa. The importance of supporting football clubs has been seen to have a profound impact on fans' behaviour and social being. Football is shown to transcend the realm of sport to influence most aspects of a fan's life and is therefore a vital and fertile ground for social research. Therefore, sport fandom should not be looked at as a mere pastime, but as a serious activity that forms an integral part of a fan's life, particularly in an African context.

Chapter III

Till Death Do Us Part: Football as Part of Everyday Life amongst Dynamos Football Club Fans in Zimbabwe

Introduction

The chapter demonstrates the nexus between social identity and supporting a football club. Drawing on concepts of social identity, it highlights how supporting a football club operates to constitute an important part of individuals' social identities. There is something more to supporting a football team besides entertainment. Supporting a football team is a kind of marriage, a commitment between the team and fans similar to 'till death do us part'. I question why such strong ties, bonds and commitment between the team and fans exist and why they last for a long time. Dynamos Football Club in Zimbabwe offers a good example of how fans form indispensable attachments to clubs even in times where there is no success. The club is the most successful team in post independence Zimbabwe winning the majority of league championships since 1980. Between 1999 and 2007, the team was not very successful, avoiding relegation on the last day of the 2005 season yet the supporters remained loyal to the club.

The supporters proved the main stay of the club as they came in their thousands to support their team in the relegation fight. The assumption is that people support a team because of its success and in the event of failure the fans will leave. The match consists of more than the players' tactical skills; the coach's training methods or the final results of the match. It goes beyond the gates of the stadium to influence everyday life. Football matches are explained and represented in many different ways: as an allegory of life and emotions; as a drama of success and decline; as an inexplicable mystery; or as a match. Whether dusty playing fields, provincial stadiums, or high-tech 'sports domes', football pitches offer arenas not only for the match, but also for the production of public spheres and imaginary spaces where social, cultural and political praxis and discourses are created, celebrated and negotiated. Football is thus played both on the pitch and beyond (Baller, 2006: 326).

This chapter provides only an exploratory understanding of Dynamos fans' commitment to their team. The Column's men were the first players of football and rugby (Giullianotti, 2004: 80). Several sports clubs had been set up by 1900 in the emerging towns catering for competition in football and other sports. In Africa, sport was a focus of struggle and resistance for colonized populations and in Bulawayo from the 1930s, the black population fought to establish control over its football system (Stuart, 1996: 167). From its colonial origins, football served as a nation-building instrument from decolonization to independence (Alegi, 2010: 56). National teams remain an important means for expressing national identities. However, beyond national identities or nation building, playing football rooted itself in African culture. By 1960s, football was an established component of African urban culture. Africans have learned, adopted and achieved a noticeable cultural appropriation of the game across the continent (Alegi, 2010: 15). Organized sport was the sole privilege of whites.

Football was particularly popular amongst new arrivals from Britain but Rhodesian schools educated boys in cricket and rugby. Football was probably introduced to blacks from 1923 by black miner workers from Transvaal migrated north to arrive in Bulawayo and Midlands to look for work and playing football in their spare time. Local Africans thus favoured football because it required little economic and cultural capital compared to other sports. Township clubs sprung up through the 1920s and 1930s, one of the oldest and most successful being the Lions Club of Bulawayo (renamed Matabeleland Highlanders in 1937) which was formed by the grandchildren of the last Ndebele king, Lobengula. Football was a venue for expressions of ethnic pride and intercultural rivalry, notably between Ndebele and Shona peoples within clubs (Giullianotti, 2004: 83).

West (2002: 1–12) notes that beginning in 1898, with an embrace of the potential inherent in the non-racial franchise, and ending in 1965 when the African elite at last renounced their fortunes in Rhodesian society for nationalism, West outlines the aspirations, disappointments and unwavering commitment of the African middle class to the achievement of respectability in colonial society. African urbanites were thus differentiated and occupied different spaces. Creation of urban identities in colonial Zimbabwe has been variously theorized showing centrality of sport especially football. Raftopoulos and Yoshikuni (1999) in the *Sites of Struggle* show there was a rich ferment of cultural, ideological, political and social activities among the African communities in the colonial urban areas which helped shape the trajectory of development at both the local, urban level and in the wider national arena.

Urban Africans were not helpless victims of economic, social and cultural hegemonic power and dominance of colonial settler society, Africans contested the colonial dispensation at every stage. Sport and in particular football was a way black people constantly strove to carve out and control their own space and lives and to blunt and mitigate the impact of colonial policies and practices as best they could under the circumstances. Ossie Stuart in his 1989s thesis entitled Good boys, footballers and strikers: African social change in Bulawayo 1933–1953 shows how sport provided as a vehicle for self-assertion of Africans during the colonial period. He was critical of the assumption that Africans were culturally helpless but highlighted through a cultural economy approach how black people were curving urban cultural spaces and football was one such important process. Ranger (2010) notes how African men in urban spaces were able to draw upon local and global forces which include sport, fashion and film among other things to create their own unique identities. He emphasises this township agency to understand how urban identities were created at this time (Ranger 2010).

Social identity and fan identities

The most substantial contributions to the study of identity have grown out of developments of social identity theory, which was pioneered by Henri Tajfel and John Turner in the 1970s. Tajfel (1972: 292) defines social identity as the individual's knowledge that he/she belongs to certain social groups together with some emotional and value significance to him/her of the group membership. The theory posits that a self-inclusive social category of some form, for example, a football team or religious affiliation, furnishes a category-congruent self-definition that forms part of the self-concept. The basic premise of this theory is that identity is formed based on group membership. Social identity is also a function of the value and emotional attachment placed on a particular group membership. Individuals strive to maintain positive social identities, which are primarily derived from favourable comparisons to group members and non-members.

Social identity theory has three primary components – categorization, identification and comparison. Categorization is when we often put others and ourselves into categories, thus it is synonymous with labelling, thus fans of a team can give themselves a label. For example, Liverpool supporters call themselves the Kop. Identification is when we associate with certain groups, which serves to bolster our self-esteem. Lastly, comparison is when we compare our groups with other groups, seeing a favourable bias towards the group we belong in the same way rival fans seem to view each other in a negative way (Uhler and Murrell, 1999). This apparent in how Dynamos fans who have positive views about each other and negative views of rival fans.

In social identity theory, the group membership is not something foreign, which is tacked onto the person; it is a real true and vital part of the person in the same way supporting a sporting team can be vital in a fan's life. Fandom can be created by the desire to be a part of the environment created by a winning team what is known as jumping on the bandwagon. Social identity theory has two processes pertaining to one becoming a fan known as BIRGing (basking in reflected glory) and CORFing (cutting off reflective failures) (Uhler and Murrell, 1999). This can explain why fans do decide to support some sporting teams because of their success. BIRGing can be defined as the tendency of individuals to publicize their connection with successful others, when they have not contributed to that success. It can thus explain why some fans might overly identify with hugely successful sporting teams. CORFing can be defined as the tendency of individuals to cut off association with failing teams; however, this aspect of the theory is debatable since most failing sporting teams have fans associated with them. The example of Dynamos fans who have remained loyal to the team in its failures also casts doubt on this aspect of the social identity theory.

Duke's (1991) distinction between a fan and a spectator is vital in trying to methodologically explain what or who can be termed a football fan. Whereas a spectator of sport will observe a spectacle and forgets it very quickly; the fan continues his/her interest until the intensity of feelings towards the team becomes so great that parts of everyday are devoted to the team. Thus, for the purpose of this research a football fan is one whose interest in the team goes beyond simply watching games but affects other part of his life. A football fan is one who sees the team as an extension of themselves such that when they talk about the team, they talk as if they are talking of themselves. In simple terms, it is someone who attends matches, knows the history and symbols of the team, has fond memories of past matches, and remembers the first match they attended and talks passionately about the team.

Football and social identity

Many studies in Europe, North and South America have shown that supporting a sports team fosters a sense of group identity. With the growing complexity and fragmentation of the modern and postmodern society sociologists have postulated that the social worlds and opportunities for collective identity in sport raise it to a higher level of social importance. Indeed identification with a sports team can provide people with an important identity prop; a source of 'we-feeling' and a sense of belonging in what would otherwise be an isolated existence (Dunning, 1988).

It seems reasonable to suggest, therefore, that fandom comprises more than simply attending and observing a sporting event. Rather, being a fan represents an association from which the individual derives considerable emotional and value significance. According to MacClancy (1996: 2), 'sport in general and football in particular are vehicles of identity, providing people with a sense of difference and a way of classifying themselves and others, whether latitudinally or hierarchically'. More specifically, they argue that ultimately a football match offers an expressive support for the affirmation of collective identity and local, regional and national antagonisms.

Supporting a particular football team not only facilitates a feeling of shared identity with fellow supporters, it also acts as a means of differentiating oneself from other groups (Jenkins, 1996). In many cases, identification with a particular team indicates what or who one is, and equally importantly, what or who they are not. In Northern Ireland, supporting particular soccer teams allows these fans to express their opposition to rival identities whilst celebrating their own. Football teams can operate as anchors of meaning via their role as vehicles through which individuals and groups can strengthen their attachment and identification with a particular community (Giulianotti, 1999). Within most societies, there are a variety of means by which social identity can be expressed, yet, for many (particularly minority) groups, football can be the sole or, at least the primary, outlet for such sentiments.

Social identities are multifaceted and constructed from a relatively specific combination of ethnic, religious and political attributes, thus there is need to demonstrate the symbiotic relationship between football fandom and social identity. It is also necessary to recognize that whilst supporters of a particular club may perceive themselves to be sharing a common identity, it is likely that in reality they will differ, both in terms of which aspects of 'the club's they identify with and their interpretation of what 'the club' represents. For example, Boyle, Giulianotti, and Williams (1994: 74) emphasize 'the division that can exist between the club as a concrete institution and as an idea which is largely personified or existent through its supporters'. However, the fundamental point to be made is that, irrespective of the degree to which it does so, support of a football club does act as a vehicle through which the other elements of an individual's identity can be affirmed and articulated.

In Africa, numerous studies have shown how football acts as an important identity marker. It has been argued that the intensity of emotional involvement in soccer is overwhelming. Alegi (2002: 17) quotes a confession from Chief Albert Luthuli's autobiography: 'I became a compulsive football fan. To this day I am carried away helplessly by the excitement of a soccer match'. Football's first introduction in Africa traced to the 1860s, by the British in South Africa. Football is thus a colonial product in Africa and has become an important aspect for most societies (Giulianotti & Armstrong, 2004). In the cities, football provides a personally pleasing leisure experience and a healthy social pastime, albeit temporary escape from the personal hazards of African city-life. Bill Murray (1994) acknowledges that the practice of soccer is a cultural form in Africa, the most important of which is the nature and practice soccer fandom. He argues that soccer has always been regarded as the game of the people and attracts their participation, which ranges from moderate involvement to committed and animated identification.

Findings and discussion

Background to Dynamos Football Club

The history of Dynamos is contested as there is aBut contest occur even where there are written records. on the team. This is characteristic of most clubs in Zimbabwe due to the lack of academic interest on the history of clubs. In the case of Dynamos, Chiweshe (2011) has shown how they are multiple and often contested origins of the club. The club was formed in 1963 in then Salisbury (now the capital city Harare). The formation of the club coincided with increased efforts of the Black Nationalist movement seeking independence. Northern Rhodesia under colonial rule practised a form of racial apartheid that led to the segregation in all walks of life including football. This meant black people were not allowed in the upper echelons of local soccer and thus relegated to the zonal township SADAFA amateur league.

Mutungamiri (1998) shows how radical white players and administrators in 1961 called for a formation of a multi racial league with two black teams from Salisbury, namely Salisbury City and United which however collapsed at the end of 1962 due to financial constraints. The players from the two black Salisbury teams were left in the cold but they continued to meet and train at the Number 5 Grounds in Harare Township (now Mbare, National). This was made easier since most of them worked together at Tobacco Sales Floor in the industrial site near Harare Township. These players then organized a match against Salisbury Yellow Peril, a team which was the best in the Salisbury Amateur League.

The group could not play without an identity; thus one of the players, a certain Nercasio Murambiwa, having heard of Dinamo Kiev in Russia, suggested the name Dynamos. Sam

Dauya who was the club's first secretary then liaised with Ken Walker who was Operations Manager at the Sales Floor, and the name was endorsed in consultation with other players. According to Mutungamiri (1998), Dauya and Walker have to be credited with founding the club. Chiweshe (2011) highlights how one of the first players disagreed with this arguing that Walker only played a peripheral role. The new club enjoyed huge success in its first match with huge crowds turning up which alarmed the colonial authorities who suspected it as a front for political parties and Dauya claimed that he was harassed at odd hours by security agents of the colonial government (Mutungamiri, 1998). With time the club would grow to become the most successful and supported clubs in post colonial Zimbabwe.

Fandom as part of everyday life

Social identity theory notes that group membership is not something foreign, which is tacked onto the person; it is a real true and vital part of the person in the same way supporting a sporting team can be vital in a fan's life. Whilst it is acknowledged that for some people (both players and spectators), sporting competition is sought purely for its intrinsic value, it is equally important to recognize that for many others, sport, and in particular football, plays a far more significant role in their lives (Armstrong and Giulianotti, 1997). The psychological and emotional effects of fandom might seem purely individualistic, but they do affect the social being in a number of ways. Emotional attachment to the team was shown by the intense sadness participants felt when the team lost and happiness when it won.

The team becomes a part of everyday life determining the fan's mood and sociability. The way the team performs determined how the participants related to friends and family to an extent that one respondent noted how his children avoid him when the team loses. He notes: '*When the team loses I am not the best person to be around. My children avoid me as I can snap at them for no apparent reason.*' For one fan, the emotional attachment to the club is to such an extent that he cries when the team loses. The importance of supporting a team was also shown by the lengths participants would go to watch the team playing. Some participants noted actually including money for games in their monthly budgets. One participant highlights that:

> *There is very little I will not do to ensure that I go and watch the team play. At times I have to go hungry at work to save lunch money for games. It is a huge thing to go games. I remember at one time I had to sell my clothes to raise money and watch a game.*

The commitment of participants is in most cases similar though differences could be noted especially due to the residential area in which one lived or grew up in. Those participants who grew up in Mbare seemed to be more committed to the team than those who grew up in other parts of the country. This was also highlighted by an elderly respondent who argued that:

> *Dynamos has always meant more to those who grew up in Harare especially Mbare. The team is linked to Mbare as its history and roots are here. The team belongs first to Mbare then to the rest of Zimbabwe.*

The emotional investment a fan places into a sporting team can have negative effects on the social being as shown by participants who displayed anti-social behaviour.

Some participants claimed that they engaged in such anti-social behaviour as destroying property, beating up rival fans and one participants who beats up his wife and children, in most instances the commitment to the team becomes so deep that the fan is unable to support another team in that particular sport and context. From the focus group discussions, a respondent noted that:

> I have seen many friends act in a bad way after a defeat. It is painful especially when we feel the players were not giving their best or the coach got tactics wrong. Defeat feels like the end of the world. Other people I know have had high blood pressure because of defeats. There are many times in the past that we have thrown stones and bottles on the pitch leading to problems with the police. Other times we have waited for the team bus to leave the stadium and we vandalise it. Other times there are skirmishes and fights with opposition fans.

Another fan highlights how defeat leads to great despair. He notes:

> I feel great sadness when the team is defeated. I feel betrayed by the team. It feels as if I found my wife in bed with another man. I am so hurt and angry that at times I cannot even eat. Defeat leaves a lump in my mouth. At times I have to feign illness not to go to work to avoid getting into fights with workmates who support other teams.

Making sense of the loss often requires finding a scapegoat to blame for the defeat. The blame usually is laid on the referees, coaches and administration. The psychological satisfaction that people gain from 'football' victories, related media coverage, social events, wearing the respective team colours and identifying with the emblems and symbols, which represent the history of the club as well as everyday realities of the fans, is immense. A victory for one young respondent was:

> … *the best thing in the world. A victory is sweet especially against our greatest rivals Caps United. We feel good with a victory. It changes everything and we are proud of the team. It feels like a personal victory against haters of my team. I know my week will be alright since I will not have any stress.*

Victory is personalized and success or failure of the team is reflected on the individual. It is such that support of the team is linked to psychological state of mind. The football team becomes an extension of the self. Its failures and successes are reflected in a personal manner such that a victory or defeat has more consequences than a mere sporting result. Outward show of happiness with a victory manifests in varied ways amongst the fans. For example one participant highlighted that: '*Since 1982 I have always bought my family a chicken1 when Dynamos win even during harsh economic conditions.*' Victory thus has profound meaning for most fans as another married participant confessed that:

> *After a victory I am more liberal with my money on such days. I buy a lot of gifts for my family. I also usually make love to my wife. There is no love making when the team loses. Actually after a defeat my children go to sleep early to avoid me.*

Five participants who were not married claimed that it would be a late night because they would drink the night away as they celebrated a victory. Another participant claimed that a victory would make him so happy that he would give the players he meets in the street presents or money. He noted:

After a win we usually give money, any amount you have to players to show our appreciation. We usually give them money at the stadium but also on the streets days following the game if we meet the players.

For another participant, sleep is peaceful when the team wins as a victory would make him forget all his problems. He notes: '*Victory especially against Caps United or Highlanders gives me a natural high, which is like being drunk with alcohol.*' Participants in the focus group discussions highlighted that being part of a celebrating crowd made them forget the problems in their everyday lives. Football thus provides an escape from everyday problems. The 'feel good' factor that victory brings is celebrated in various ways such as being generous to friends and families.

Happiness associated with victory requires overt manifestation, for example, a respondent claimed that: '*When Dynamos wins everyone in my neighbourhood knows because I play my favourite records at a high volume. I sing like there is no tomorrow.*' For fans, there is thus a direct correlation between happiness and victory. Behaviour of fans after matches corresponds to the result at the weekend. Another fan pointed out how:

Since the 1980s I have celebrated a victory by buying my wife a new piece of house ware or a present for her. She has many glasses, plates and chinaware because of Dynamos. However when the team loses it is the opposite. I do not like talking to people and my wife knows it's best to just leave me alone.

Married participants in the focus group discussions noted that they would indulge their wives and children with niceties such as chicken and ice creams in the event of a victory. The participants talked as if they were part of the team. They did not speak of the team as a different entity to themselves, for example, the constant use of the phrase, '*when we win, I am happy.*' Happiness of most participants during the season is directly linked to the results on the weekend. Personalization of defeat and victory means the team becomes the anchor of social identity. One is a *muDembare* (Dynamos fan) first then everything else later. The team controls and influences almost all parts of an individual's life to the extent that even missing a single game is difficult. An example is 74 years old who claimed that he had rarely missed a home game since the 1980s. He indicated:

> *For over twenty years I have been committed to this team. I am here almost every game. I have seen the good and the bad days. It is part of my life and it is my everything. I can only miss a game for something serious like a funeral. When I do not have money, I visit my son Sunday morning and he automatically knows that I want money for the game.*

Most games are played on Sunday which provides challenges for those fans who are church goers. Such fans noted that at church, it was known that they go to watch football so they were not expected to participate in after church activities. One fan highlighted:

> *I had to quit choir because it coincided with time to go and watch Dynamos. I pray and attend church and ask God to guide my team but I cannot be there all day. I have a friend who lives in Kuwadzana (suburb which is over an hour from stadium) who attends church services in Mbare (where the stadium is located) so that it would be easier for him to attend games afterwards.*

The big games were highlighted as the most difficult to miss. In the focus group discussions, fans shared variety of stories about what they had done in the past not to miss a game against Caps United or Highlanders. One such story was narrated by a fan who noted that:

> At one time in the 1990s I had to find novel ways to leave my father in-laws funeral for a few hours to watch a game against Highlander. I lied to my wife that I was required at work to help with something for an hour. It was such a bad lie because I have never worked on Sunday but it worked.

Such importance to attending the matches extends to having one exclusive team. Similar to a real marriage, there is no room for 'cheating' (supporting or coveting other teams) the team. As such fans are loyal to this one team above all else. It is a commitment until death as one fan indicated: *'I was born a Dynamos fan, I grew up a Dynamos fan, I will die a Dynamos fan and God willing in heaven I will be a Dynamos fan.'* Even when the team is not performing or winning anything, fans kept on supporting with all participants claiming that they would continue even if the team was relegated to lower divisions. A female respondent stated that:

> I would rather stop supporting football if Dynamos were disbanded than to support another team since I signed a blood contract with the team that cannot be easily broken. It is unthinkable. I actually feel it was a sin that not even God will forgive. Even if they lose I will be here supporting. 'Amai havaraswe chero vaka hura' (you do not throw away your mother because she is a prostitute).

Another fan claimed that:

Even if it were five year olds dressed in blue called Dynamos I would still support them. It does not matter who is playing. What matters are the team and its symbols and not the players. Great players have come and gone but the team still remains.

All the respondents agreed that their love for the team was a marriage that could only be broken by death and leaving Dynamos was unthinkable, as one fan aptly pointed out: '*With this team it is till death do us part. Nothing will come between our love for this team.*'

MuDembare: in group identities among Dynamos fans

Tafjel (1972) argues that members of a group have a positive view of other group members whilst having negative view of members of other rival groups. The participants in the research showed that they had a positive bias towards fellow fans, whilst having a negative view of rival fans. The participants tended only to highlight the negative aspects of rival fans especially fans of Caps United and Highlanders. For example, the participants claimed that: 'Caps United supporters are not true fans because they tend abandon their team when it is doing badly whilst Highlanders fans are violent' (focus group discussion, 11 July 2005, Sunningdale). The expression of social identity requires reference to both the groups, that is, to which an individual belongs and to those he/she does not. A consequence of this is the construction of in group–out group consciousness. To explain why Caps United and Highlanders fans are the most disliked by Dynamos fans, one has to look at the history of the league in Zimbabwe and the ethnic composition of the teams especially Highlanders. The capital city Harare witnesses the country's biggest derby between Caps United and Dynamos. Caps United, as the other successful team in Harare has won a host of cup competitions, provides biggest rivals to Dynamos in Harare and this has created a dislike between the fans of the two clubs. The interesting part about this rivalry is that the teams usually play on different days thus when, for example, Dynamos faces another team, Caps United fans come to support that team and vice versa.

There is a special camaraderie among the fans especially at away games. Fans have formed many friendships with people they met at the games. Participants in focus groups noted the idea that Dynamos supporters refer to each other as muDembare. One respondent said that though they may disagree about who should play for the team ultimately they all agreed on what the team needs to achieve. Another respondent claimed that Dynamos fans have grown in the game unlike Highlanders fans who he claims turn violent when they lose at home. This respondent argued that Dynamos fans are not violent but may be forced to defend themselves. Another respondent noted that it was the same with fans in other cities. The respondent claimed that once he was beaten up in Bulawayo by Highlanders fans and was helped by other Dynamos fans who took him to the hospital yet they were Ndebele and he has been friends with them since.

Participants noted how Monday morning is interesting at work or schools as fans mock each other depending on how their teams play. The history of the derby is littered with violent episodes when fans have turned to fist fights. The battle for Harare (Caps United vs. Dynamos) is interesting given the differences in the number of fans each team attracts for their games. Dynamos have the larger crowds but Caps United fans make this up by being more vocal than their counterparts. Caps

United and Highlanders fans are seen as enemies thus they had a song they sing about the two teams which says that: 'pane team mbiri dzandakamaka. Kepe kepe neHighlander' (they are two teams that I hate, Caps United and Highlanders). Other fans accused Highlanders supporters because they are violent and he was once beaten up at Barbourfields (Highlanders home ground in Bulawayo). With Caps United fans, the bone of contention was who the best in Harare was while with Highlanders it was about the best nationally with serious ethno-regional tones. Highlanders is largely viewed as 'team yemandebele' (team of the Ndebele) by the focus group participants. Since 1980, when the country gained independence competition for supremacy in the league has been between the three big teams (Dynamos, Caps United and Highlanders), though teams such as Amazulu, Motor Action, Black Aces and Zimbabwe Saints have at one time won the league championship. Caps United, as the other successful team in Harare has won a host of cup competitions, provides biggest rivals to Dynamos in Harare and this has created a dislike that is apparent to this day demonstrated when these teams play. With Highlanders, it was also about dominance at national level but it goes deeper than football.

Dynamos fans in this research claimed that Highlanders fans hate them because they think Dynamos is related to ZANU PF, whom the Ndebele blame for the Gukurahundi (episode in the 1980s which saw the army killing many people in Matebeleland region) killings. The participants further claimed that Highlanders fans are tribalists and very violent at Barbourfields especially when their team loses. The participants claimed that there were many numerous reports of beatings of Dynamos fans at that stadium. One has to look at the colonial period to also understand this dislike exacerbated by the colonial policy of divide and rule. This led to animosity between the different tribal groups. The support base for Highlanders is mainly in Matebeleland and among the Ndebele, whilst Dynamos tends to have a larger spread of support base but mainly in Mashonaland and Manicaland. This link between ethnicity and fandom in Zimbabwe is more complex than space allows in this chapter. This is because they are many Ndebele people who support Dynamos and many non Ndebele fans of Highlanders. Not all Ndebeles and Shonas support similar teams or like football for that matter. Dynamos itself was largely formed by people of Malawian background. Thus, ethnic basis of both clubs requires a nuanced and contextualised analysis. What is important however is to note how football remains an important configuration in the identity of those who support the clubs.

Conclusion

This chapter has highlighted the extent to which Dynamos Football Club has been and continues to be used by various social groups and individuals for the expression of certain elements of their identities. It has shown how football clubs play a significant part in people's lives. In such incidences, sport has eschewed its desired apolitical nature and has been inextricably bound up with the politics of division as rival fans view each other as enemies. It is evident that football provides an arena for these processes at regional, national and international level, yet in this instance the emphasis has been on relatively specific local context with Dynamos Football Club being the focal point of the research. It can be concluded that though some differences could be noted between fans in different age groups, all fans are similar in their love and loyalty for the team and their dislike for rival teams. Whilst studies of football fandom have proved a popular source of enquiry within the sociology of sport, there is still a great deal of further research that can be done in this area, especially in Africa. The importance of supporting football clubs was shown to have a profound impact on fans' behaviour and social being. Football is shown to transcend the realm of sport to influence most aspects of a fan's life and is therefore a vital and fertile ground for social research. Sport fandom in Africa should not be looked at as a mere pastime, but as a serious activity that forms an integral part of a fan's life. Football fandom is intrinsically linked with how people view themselves. In many ways, teams determine happiness and sadness of many fans in Africa. In this way, the power of the soccer on the continent cannot over emphasized. The game goes beyond the 90 minutes on the pitch, weaving its way beyond the mundane. Supporting a football team is a commitment of heart and soul. A marriage of sorts based on imagined communities of fans sharing in the successes and failures of their sporting heroes.

Chapter IV

Football Rivalries in Zimbabwe

Introduction

This chapter provides an analysis of how sport (football in particular) can be an arena to cement, reproduce and celebrate historical conflicts. It questions the simplistic assumptions of a growing field of sports for development which views football as a vehicle for social development. Using football rivalries in Zimbabwe as an example, the chapter highlights how sport can be a vehicle of playing out conflicts and passing rivalries from one generation to the next. The chapter explores the intertwined historical, political, ethno-regional among other causes of rivalries reflecting how football reproduces underlying fractures that exist in society.

Football rivalries provide the dark side of sport and highlight how often sport can be a vehicle of hate. Marsh and Frosdick (2005: 5) contend that 'the game of football has been associated with violent rivalry since its beginnings in 13th century England. Medieval football matches involved hundreds of players, and were essentially pitched battles between the young men of rival villages and towns – often used as opportunities to settle old feuds, personal arguments and land disputes.' Guilanotti (2001) argues that, one aspect of football that has been globalised is the notion of football rivalry.

Ligion (2007) notes that football fandom in Africa is very much related to the kinship ties prevalent in the region. The oldest teams have generated supported among local Africans that is expressed in family terms as a bond between the current generation and their ancestors who founded these cultural institutions, making football clubs "family". Beyond representing family ties, teams in many regions represent ethnic and tribal groups, often highlighting and sometimes exacerbating tensions that sit right below the surface. The worst soccer disaster in African History occurred in Accra Ghana during a match between Rivals Accra Hearts of Oak Sporting Club and Asante Kitoko. According to Fridy and Bobby (2009) the Hearts and Kitoko Rivalry is usually inflamed by the inherent nexus between football and politics in lieu of the relationship between Ghana's dominant two soccer clubs, Accra Hearts of Oak and Asante Kitoko and Ghana's dominant political parties the National Democratic Party and the New Patriotic Party. In this context soccer rivalry is being used to reflect on test political dichotomies and afflictions in society.

For Grooves (2011) the long time success of rival clubs further amplify the rivalry, for example, Al Ahly and Zamalek won all but one of the league titles between 1949 and 1962. Today games between the two teams results in noticeably less foot and car traffic in Cairo. The rivalry has sometimes resulted in destruction and death, to the extent of forcing the cancelation of the entire league in the early 1970s (Grooves, 2011). The Egyptian government has gone so far as to situate the game at neutral venues, and to import foreign officials when the two rivals clash, to prevent partiality and claims to it. Last (2004) did a study about football rivalry in Eritrea. For Last (2004) Eritrean football rivalry is most linked with the strong historical divides between Christian and Muslim populations. He goes on to note that for some time the two most successful football clubs in Eritrea were the Muslim supported Mar Rosso FC and the Christian supported Hamasein FC, the rivalry between these two teams was fierce to the extent of straining the fragile peace between Muslims and Christians.

The Harare Derby: When the city turns blue or green

The capital city Harare witnesses the country's biggest derby between Caps United and Dynamos F.C. Caps, as the other successful team in Harare has won a host of cup competitions, and thus the biggest rivals to Dynamos in Harare. This has created a dislike between the fans of the two clubs. The interesting part about this rivalry is that the teams usually play on different days thus when for example Dynamos faces another team, Caps fans come to support that team and vice versa. Respondents from both teams noted how Monday morning is interesting at work or schools as fans chide each other depending on how their teams played. The history of the derby is littered with violent episodes when fans have turned to fist fights. The battle for Harare is interesting given the differences in the number of fans each team attracts for their games. Dynamos have the larger crowds but Caps United fans make this up by being more vocal than their counterparts. One Caps United fan on being mocked about Dynamos having more fans than his team, retorted that '*Chero nhunzi dzikawanda sei hadzigadzire huchi*' (no matter how many there are, flies will never make honey).

Rivalry between Caps United and Dynamos has according to fans from both clubs intensified to eclipse the Highlanders-Dynamos duel. Proximity of fans that interact with each other in Harare daily ensures that at work places, schools and homes. Caps Rovers (as it was known then) was promoted into the earned top-flight league status in 1976 (Sharuko 2011). Pharmaceutical company Caps Holdings later bankrolled it. It became popularly known as the Manchester Road Boys in reference to where the company is situated in Harare. The team over the years became famous for winning cup competitions and they were coined Cup Kings. The company later on sold the team to Twine Phiri who later sold the club to Farai Jere. The team drew many fans because of its success and style brought by being bankrolled by a large company. A significant number of first generation fans of *Kepe kepe bhora* (Caps is football) supported the team because they hated the dominance of Dynamos in Harare. The team offered an alternative from the already established team. Caps also had an appeal for middle class fans that saw themselves as better than the large number of poor classes that followed Dynamos. This aspect of the team was confirmed by two old fans who remember a time in the late 1980s where there was a popular saying that one needed to have five O' levels (educational qualifications required then to get a job) to support the team.

Sharuko (2011) offers an analysis of the first derby in 1976 through the eyes of now famous football commentator Charles Mabika who was at the game. Mabika noted, 'Rufaro was filled to capacity that day and although CAPS Rovers were not as popular as they are today, they had a sizeable backing and you also had a lot of Black Aces fans throwing their support behind the new boys, Aces were Dynamos' bogey team then but they had started to go down and CAPS Rovers were on the up so a lot of Aces fans, who really enjoyed seeing Dynamos suffer, appeared to be shifting into the CAPS corner.' Through continued success and brilliant players such as Shackman Tauro, Joel "Jubilee" Shambo, Stanford "Stix" Mtizwa and Stanley Ndunduma the team attracted more and more fans.

Over the years the Green Machine as Caps are now popularly known as, has forged a fierce rivalry with Dynamos that brings out a lot of emotions among fans in within the capital when the game comes. 2011 witnessed the 67th Harare derby and fans from both teams interviewed agree that the level of football has gone down but the sentiment and magic of the terraces still remain.

The derby has had its fair share of ugly scenes that fans remember. Violence and hooliganism are never far away where emotions run high. Fans particularly remember a match at Rufaro Stadium celebrating 100 years for Harare in the 1990s which ended prematurely when Dynamos walked off the pitch in protest against Caps making too many substitutions. The ensuing running battles between rival fans and police led to many injuries especially from the teargas used to control crowds. Fights are a common occurrence especially when a fan sits among rivals. For regular stadium goers it is taboo to wear blue amongst Caps fans and to wear green among Dynamos fans. Wearing the wrong colors can lead to beatings. It is such scenes and behavior patterns that keep away families from matches and ensures that rich upper and middle classes shun stadiums. Through observation, the behavior of some fans after matches is dangerous as they celebrate or find their way home. Some hang precariously from buses and moving cars. The noise of cars as they continuously hoot with flags flying is another unique feature of the post-match fan experience in Zimbabwe.

Battle of Zimbabwe: Football and ethnicity in Dynamos versus Highlanders

Often described by Robson Sharuko, editor of The Herald in Zimbabwe as the Battle of Zimbabwe; matches between Highlanders and Dynamos are about dominance at national level but it goes deeper than football. Dynamos fans in this research claimed that Highlanders fans hate them because they think Dynamos is related to ZANU PF, whom the Ndebele blame for the Gukurahundi massacres in the late 1980s. The rivalry takes an ethnic, cultural and political dimension. A Dynamos fan claimed that Highlanders fans are tribalists and very violent at Barbourfields especially when their team loses. However a Highlanders fan asked in this research also accused Dynamos fans of being tribalists who think they are superior to everyone else.

Another Highlanders fan was of the views that Dynamos and ZANU PF are the same entity given that they were formed the same year and the influence of politicians such as Webster Shamu at the team. Thus all in Matabeleland must hate Dynamos, like ZANU PF according to this fan. There is a complex interplay of factors in choosing a team to support that it would be wrong to generalise all Highlanders supporters as Ndebele and all Dynamos fans as Shona. I have come across many Shona people who support Highlanders and the team has a huge following in Harare as seen when they play in the city. Dynamos also have a strong loyal base in Bulawayo. Though ethnicity plays an important part in football in Zimbabwe, it is not the only determining factor. Chiweshe (2011) has shown that Dynamos fans are drawn from different ethnic groups and defy any singular ethnic definition.

Violence is an important feature to this rivalry. The respondents claimed that there were many numerous incidents of beatings of rival fans, with one respondent claiming that he is a victim of one such beating. One has to look at the colonial period to also understand this dislike which was exacerbated by the colonial policy of divide and rule. This led to animosity between the different ethnic groups. Football as an enactment of physical superiority and prowess has played a significant part in such ethnic battles where players are made to feel as if they are representing something bigger than a mere football team. The ethnicity of the players however does not matter, once they put on the team's jersey they are seen as part of group. From fieldwork carried in this project and my many years following Zimbabwean football, I can argue that ethnic identity is closely linked to supporting Highlanders. At the turn of the century, when the team dominated the league for four years, the Bosso (nickname for Highlanders) road show (hordes of fans in their black and white regalia) would invade all towns when the team was playing. The team represents more than football but an important part of being Ndebele male. This idea is passed to younger generations by old fans, transmitted through taking them to games. At one time the Soweto stand at Barbourfields was notorious for people being beaten up for failing to speak in Ndebele.

Mining towns and small town fan identities

Since independence Zimbabwe has had many teams hailing from small towns especially in mining areas. These teams, owned by parent mining companies such as Hwange Colliery, Shabanie Mine, Mimosa, Ziscosteel and Lancashire Steel. Football was and remains an important part of these mining towns. From the days of Rio Tinto or even the romance of *Tanganda* and residents of Mutare; football teams become the heartbeat and symbol for small and mining towns. The teams represent an identity for residents in mine compounds, an aspiration for young boys and heroes for local communities. A young fan from Shabanie Mine remembers how at the turn of the century when the team got into the premier league players such as Thomas *(Chaurura)* Makwasha, Asani Juma and Francis *(Gweje-gweje)* Chandida became cult heroes at the mine. Home games at Maglas Stadium[1] were eagerly awaited by the whole community and on match day the town came to stand still.

Football remains an important fabric of the community especially after the asbestos mine closed. The game became an escape for many people who were out of work even when the team was relegated in 2006. The team was promoted into the league again in 2010 but the emergence of Platinum Stars (formerly known as Mimosa) in 2011 led to a new rivalry. This rivalry is in many ways linked to the fortunes of the mining companies controlling the teams. Shabanie Mine has faced many financial and operational difficulties leading to many workers being laid off whilst Platinum Mine has flourished. The social tensions in the suburbs of Zvishavane are often played out on the soccer field.

The importance of football and sport to a mining town cannot be under estimated. Yet the economic meltdown post 2000 has negatively affected many mining towns leading to the death of many mining teams. Torwood *'Mugomba'* Stadium in Redcliff was a symbol of hope and inspiration for the mining community from the 70's through to the mid 90's when Ziscosteel F.C. was one of the country's best soccer teams with

---

[1] Allegedly named after a white mine manager who wore spectacles (*maglass* as known by locals).

players such as players like the late Ephraim Dzimbiri and Paul Gundani. The decline of the mine and the team left a void that can still be felt in the town as Jason Moyo writing in the Mail and Guardian on August 17 2011 noted, 'In the radio commentary box above the deserted Torwood Stadium, which overlooks the steel factory, I moan about the demise of our local football team, which used to play in the premiership league until the factory began collapsing.' There is hope for the town as in August 2011 government of Zimbabwe launched a new Ziscosteel and maybe the good times will be back to Redcliff.

Conclusion

Football rivalries form an important part of the football fan experience in Zimbabwe. This chapter has provided a context of understanding football rivalries. It focused on some of the most enduring rivalries. The chapter shows that football rivalries are based on a complex interplay of class, gender, ethnic, geographical location, race, age and citizenship differences. In intercity rivalries this is more complex given that members of a single household can have deep allegiances to rival teams. Rivalries often turn violent and they are played out within and without the stadium.

Chapter V

One of the Boys: Female Fans Responses to Masculine and Phallocentric Nature of Football Stadiums

Introduction

Studies of football fandom from across the world all highlight masculine and misogynistic tendencies of the football stadiums. The domination of males in football spaces makes stadiums hostile environments for women who are often physically and verbally abused. This chapter outlines the experiences of female fans who attend matches in Zimbabwe. It provides a nuanced analysis of female fans' responses to the masculine and phallocentric nature of the football stadium. In Zimbabwe women fans are increasing in number, challenging the dominant believe that stadiums are no-go areas for women. Using in-depth interviews and focus group discussions with forty female fans, the chapter highlights how women react, negotiate and respond to misogynistic and vulgar songs and chants. This research in Zimbabwe brings to the fore the voices of female fans and how they construct the stadium experience. The chapter draws from in-depth interviews and focus group discussions to highlight how female fans cope with masculine nature of stadiums. Women use various strategies such as joining in the singing, remaining oblivious, sitting in quieter parts of the stadium and responding to abusers.

The presence of women in largely male dominated spaces such as football stadiums offers interesting questions about the paradoxical nature of female fandom. This chapter focuses on how part of the female fan experience in football stadium using women who attend matches in Harare, Zimbabwe. Scholars (Agnew 2006; Jones 2008; Gosling 2007) from across the world have shown how football stadiums are punctuated by abusive, misogynistic and phallocentric images. As such they are highly female unfriendly yet the number of women fans is increasing across the world. The question is how then do women respond to the abusive and denigrating atmosphere of football stadiums? What mechanisms do they use to survive the misogynistic attacks from male fans? Using a sample of forty purposively sampled fans, this chapter offers an exploratory endeavor into understanding how female fans respond to masculine cultures that dominate football stadiums.

The research begins from the standpoint that female fans are not a homogenous or special group. They are differentiated in the same manner as male fans and are attracted to football for varied reasons. This study thus avoids essentialising female fans or depicting them as anything but any other ordinary fans. In this chapter I highlight how they negotiate stadium spaces, which are intrinsically sexist. There are many female fandoms that explain why women respond to sexism within the stadium in different ways. The importance of this chapter is that it highlights the need for a serious analysis of stadiums in Zimbabwe to ensure that teams attract more fans and provide an environment that makes football accessible to everyone.

Patriarchal nature of fandom

The male dominance and misogyny that characterises football stadiums unconsciously re-establishes soccer as pathology of patriarchy meaning a misogynistic, male-oriented tradition that excludes women (Heide 1978). This exclusion of women is also apparent in the thinness of research on women as serious fans in their own right. There is limited research about female fans especially where males still largely dominate public spaces. Women however also love football and are as fanatic as their male counterparts. Studies on female fans in Germany, Italy and the United Kingdom, show that despite their minority status women are just as enthusiastic and devoted male fans (Toffoletti and Mewett 2012). Football fandom has proved a fertile ground for the display of masculine identities a readymade arena for the playing out of these identities. Sexual symbols and phallocentric images permeate football fan cultures. Football songs and chants in Zimbabwe are punctuated with many misogynistic messages, which celebrate male sexual domination.

The songs degrade women and perceive sport as a sexual encounter in which the losing team is portrayed as a woman. The stadium is thus a theatre for asserting male dominance. Watching games - especially in the stadium, as opposed to at home - is a predominantly male pursuit. Armstrong (1998), in his study of football hooliganism, found that only 10% of fans at Sheffield United FC games were female, and there is no reason to believe that this percentage would differ substantially elsewhere (certainly, the anecdotal, visual evidence of televised soccer matches indicates as much). In part moreover, the fact that fans will be in close and sometimes uncomfortable physical proximity - also marks them as traditionally gender-inappropriate for women. In Zimbabwe stadiums are predominantly male arenas where virtues of masculinity are celebrated and reinforced. The language and symbols of these spaces are phallocentric and highly misogynistic.

Soccer fandom is traditionally a patriarchal institution, which effectively serves the reproduction of hegemonic masculinity and allows little room for women, because femininity is constructed as an object of sexual conquest and physical inferiority. From the description of scoring as a sexual act and losing team being likened to whore (vagina more precisely), sexist symbols are part and parcel of fandom (Chiweshe 2011). Football stadiums provide an arena in which masculinity is constructed around a clear and distinct set of defining norms. The stadium was in the past not considered a place for 'upright females.' This chapter shows that this view persists today among soccer fans in Zimbabwe, highlighting how football fandom recreates and reinforces the perceived inferiority of women. The heavily masculine nature of football teams fosters a culture of misogynistic behavior that makes young players see themselves as powerful and privileged, and anyone else – including women – as lesser objects (Gosling 2007). Exaltation of manhood is part of football in Zimbabwe. The songs and chants tell a story of masculine domination of an opponent which is feminised. Feminisation of opposing teams is a vital part of watching and supporting football. The dominant gender regime in football thus remains highly masculine. Fandom promotes an orthodox form of masculinity that promotes negative (sexist, misogynistic, and anti-female) attitudes toward women.

Women fans from across the world

The misogynistic treatment of female fans, players or administrators in stadiums seems to transcend national borders. Women's relationship with soccer is often fraught with contestations of female invasion of male spaces. Caudwell

(1999) for example argues that for women 'playing football, an activity clearly constructed as male, affects players' subjectivity, in particular their gender identity.' Football construction as a male space thus affects how female players define themselves. This is also true for female fans that are forced to define their fan identities juxtaposed to this hostility towards them. What is interesting in Caudwell's study is how some female players were able to use football to 'invert sexual norms' and challenge heterosexual femininity. As women penetrate male spaces they also begin to reconfigure and reorient specific identities about their personhood. As I focus on responses of female fans in Zimbabwe, it is interesting to note some women to question hegemonic narratives about femininity use how being a fan as a vehicle. By coming to stadiums women are challenging the male domination of sports consumption. Many male supporters as an invasion of man-only spaces and their appropriation of male powers and privileges largely view this.

Female fans have for a long time been accused of being 'fickle' or fake yet Dalpian Zylbersztejn, Batistella and Rossi (2013) shows that women have genuine bonds with their teams that define their social identities. They note that:

> ...*a strong tendency was detected by the fanatical women in assuming their identification with their club as an important facet of their personality. They use this facet as a positive interpersonal relationship facilitator or as a conflict catalyst. The belonging sentiment and the rites involving their clubs (e.g. stadium presence) appear to be important components of the interviewees' social identity...There is among the respondents and the clubs a relationship of, a certain way, sacred characteristics – that demands constant and unconditional support, geographical extrication and routine moderating effects (Dalpian et al 2013: 10).*

For Ahuvi (2005) female fans connect to their clubs in an affective ways that is intrinsic to their self-identities. Female football fans thus identify strongly with their clubs and being a fan is an integral part of how they define themselves. Yet Anderson (2007) shows that female American football spectators are often addressed as ignorant girlfriends, wives, friends, daughters, sisters and mothers of all-knowing male viewers. Women thus constantly have to defend their 'fan credentials' whilst navigating male dominated spaces.

Curi (2008) shows how women were an integral part of the contingent of Brazilian fans that were at the 2006 Germany World Cup. In Norway, football remains the most popular sport for females in general and for female youth in particular, yet representation of women as players or fans remains unequal (Skille 2008). In Israel Ben-Porat (2009: 883) notes that: 'The (male) Israeli spectator is likely to believe that football is a man's game and the presence of 'the other sex' in the terraces is unnatural: What the hell is she doing in the stadium?' Men feel as if they own the game and the stadiums. Stadiums have been created and recreated as male domains where women can appear in prescribed roles such as wives, girlfriends, mothers or sisters of the players. Most male fans dispute the genuine female fan, in love with football across the world. Moreira (2013) blames this stereotyping of women as 'fake fans' on sex typing of sports within Western culture in which sport is constructed as a masculinised activity. Pfister, Lenneis and Mintert (2013) argue that female football fans who go to stadiums will suffer a measure of sexism. Women can use a variety of ways to cope with the sexism. One way is to adopt the men's perspectives in order to be accepted as 'authentic fans.'

In Pfister et al (2013) study women reacted to men's domination in the football stadium by founding women's only fan group that allows them to find a way to be women and fans. This is a radical move, which ensures that women redefine fandom on their own terms. It allows for the emergence of other forms of fandom that are not based on patriarchal and masculine ideas. In this way women can 'occupy' certain spaces within the stadium. Erhart (2011) provides an interesting account of the fan group Ladies of Besiktas that is an all women fan club founded in 2006. The ladies support Besiktas club in Turkey and the group was formed to fight sexism in the terraces. The group marches into Besiktas's Inönü Stadium dressed in identical black and white scarves and jackets and blow whistles to mute the male fans that use vulgar language (Erhart 2011).

In a study in England, Jones (2008) interviewed 38 female fans and concluded that women use three basic strategies to cope with sexism and homophobia within stadiums. First, they expressed disgust at abuse, sometimes redefining fandom to exclude abusers. Second, they downplayed sexism. Their third strategy was to embrace gender stereotypes, arguing that femininity was inconsistent with "authentic" fandom and that abuse was a fundamental part of football (Jones 2008: 516). These strategies reflect how stadiums are created with a unique culture and set of rules based on male experiences. Women have to find ways to fit into these cultures and accept that there is a level of exclusion through sexism and degradation. One of the ways is for women to downplay misogyny.

Many female fans ignore misogynist occurrences or make light of them, even though they would never accept those same occurrences in any other part of their social life (Selmer and Sülzle 2008). Selmer (2004: 92) quotes one female 'Of course,

I've heard words like 'cunt', but not addressed to me.' Female fans are forced to rationalise abusive language to 'fit in'. The implication however is that when women accept and ignore sexist and homophobic language they become themselves part of football as a male world and accept its rules. Women cannot however question this because, 'If you as a woman on the terraces criticise sexist occurrences that might be signing off your status as fan. Discriminating comments or actions do draw a line, they invoke in- and exclusions' (Selmer and Sülzle 2008: 8). Female agency is thus limited by the need to belong, to be part of the group and to be seen as one of the boys.

Findings and discussion

Singing with the boys: Women as active agents within stadiums

Some women fans join in the singing and abusive language. One of the women indicated that it is all part of being a fan. The stadium has a unique language and culture. According to this respondent anyone who comes to the stadium should be aware of this or else they should stay away. She questioned why women should be seen as powerless victims who cannot hold their own in a men's world. Another women interviewed noted that, '*kana tauya bhora tinotoimba sevamwe kuzvinakidze. Hazvina basa kuti zvinyadzi, ndozvekubhora izvozvo. Handiti tinoimba zvemahure because ariko. Saka chinoshamisa pahure chii? Tinototukirara mareferee futi nezvamai vake. Ndokubhora kana usingade enda unogara kushade*' (when we come to the stadium it is to enjoy the whole atmosphere so we sing and dance with other supporters.

The vulgar songs do not bother me at all because it is part of football. We sing about prostitutes because they exist and

78

there is nothing special about that. If you feel offended then you can always go and watch from the expensive seats. Such women are very much part of the core group of fans that sing and dance throughout the matches. They are not at all disturbed by the nature of the language being used and its implications on constructing or demeaning female bodies.

Some women take up the role of the fan and immerse themselves in its masculine nature. They identify themselves with male fans and actually participate in singing and shouting obscenities at other women and men in the stadium. Borrowing from Caudwell's argument of female soccer players inverting sexual norms, it is clear that fans in this category are also using the stadium as a space to adopt and practice masculinities. Female fans do not see themselves as different to their male counterparts as noted by one of the research participants: *'Mukepekepe, mukepekepe hazvina basa nhengo yako yemuviri. Mukadzi kana murume supporter isupporter'* (Caps United fans are all similar whether they are men or women. Chiweshe (2012) has shown how stadiums offer a space for male supporters to use vulgar language, which they do not normally use in other public spaces. This is also true for female fans because stadiums allow them to transcend the patriarchal demands of hetero-normativity in which women are not supposed to be loud, vulgar and outspoken.

The stadium thus allows women to take up roles that in their normal lives social norms prohibit. As noted by another participant: *'kubhora tinotaura zvatinoda. Zvese zvinoita kana kutuka munhu zvinyadzi'* (we say what we want, even vulgar language). By taking up these masculine roles female fans are promoting and entrenching hegemonic ideas about women's bodies. Women's fans are thus participants in promoting the same system of misogyny that undermines gender equality and defines women narrowly as sex objects. Through a process of dissociation female fans who actively participate in promoting processes that demeans women. Such female fans are in the habit of dismissing everything feminine as weak thus within the stadium they dissociate themselves from women who are more likely to match the feminine stereotypes.

The women within this category tend to be younger and single when compared to those that had quit coming to the stadium. Whilst the sample is too small to make generalisations on the impact of age and marital status on how women respond to abuse within stadium, there is an emerging pattern that younger and single women have more space to take masculine personas within stadiums. What was also interesting from the focus group discussions was how female fans do not relate the words in the songs to themselves or other women close to them. They argued that the songs were not personal and thus were not talking about them. A research participant had this to say: *'angori masongs haana kana basa aya. Hapana zita rangu kana remunhu saka unodhiniwa nei kana pataurwa zvehure kana iwe usiri hure racho'* (they are just songs and mean nothing. It is not like we are singing people's name.

The songs may be misogynistic and portraying women as sexualised bodies. Within the confines of the stadium women can redefine their gender identities and actually attack their own gender. In the focus group it was indicated how some women actually attack players for being 'weak' like women or stating, *tavaisa* (we have sexed them) to describe beating another team. Female fans in this category also argued that not all songs are misogynistic and vulgar. They gave examples of songs that were both religious and not vulgar.

Dembare iteam, rovha ngoma usekekerere, kana ndafa musandicheme ndoenda ndoga pahukama (Dynamos is our team beat the drums and be happy, if I die do not moan, I will go alone.

Akuda kuchema asina kumborohwa (they want to cry without being beaten)

Such songs are gender neutral and allow everyone to participate and 'showed that stadiums are not always about abusing women.' Other songs noted by women fans in this category actually sexualised male bodies. The fans argued that such songs though few showed how all bodies within stadiums were sexualised. They include songs such as:

Officer mamisa mboro, officer mamisa mboro, inohaizi nguva yekumisa mboro (Policeman why is your penis erect? This is not the time to have an erect penis

Tapinda tapinda, Hemeni Baba, tapinda, tapinda haiwa Jehovha mune ngoni (We successes, Amen to the Lord who has mercy)

The argument by these female fans is that both men and women suffer from bad language and sexualisation. There was however agreement by all women that it is mostly female fans that suffer from whistles and abusive shouts such as '*hure*' (prostitute). Women in this category highlighted how they either ignore or shout back at people who shout obscenities. A fan narrated how one time part of the crowd started calling her a prostitute as she walked up the terrace and she responded, '*hure ndimai vako*' (your mother is the prostitute). Another fan noted how whistles do not bother her because she also does it when a woman with big buttocks walks by, as she argued: '*munhu akabatana akapfura hazvina kuipa kumuudza nemuridzo kuti zvinhu zvake anazvo. Even inini ndotofara maface akaridza muridzo because ndinawo maassets*' (if a nicely shaped woman passes in front of the crowd I see no problem with whistling because we are simply appreciating her shapely body. Even myself, I am happy when men whistle at me because I have the assets).

Related to the above is physical harassment of women within stadiums. All respondents generally accepted and narrated various stories of being victims of back tapping, breast fondling and assault. Such acts appear rampant in games that attract huge crowds of over twenty thousand like the big derbies. Women within this category outlined various ways in which they respond to such abuse. One of the participants narrated how she once had to slap a man who had touched her buttocks and luckily the police were near and the guy was arrested. Another noted that she always moves around with a group of male supporters so she rarely suffers this form of abuse. Being in the company of other male supporters is a form of protection against physical harassment. What was however disturbing is how some of the fans in this category found glee in narrating how women from rival teams are subjected to physical abuse outside the stadium some years ago. In this case sisterhood does not exist with female fans of rival teams as noted by Dynamos Football Club fan, '*dzetse idzetse chete rume kana hadzi ndakarimaka. Pane pandichati nekuti tiri vakadzi tashamwari nesupporter yeHighlander*' (A frog is a frog (nickname given to Caps United supporters) whether male or female I hate it. There is no way I can ever befriend a Highlander supporter just because she is a woman).

Within this category there are also women who do not necessarily join in the singing or use of bad language but condones it as a necessary part of fan culture. They believe that feminine traits are not compactable with behaviors expected to 'real' fans. One such fan noted that: '*anyone who comes to the stadium should be aware of the use of vulgar language or else they should stay away. You cannot come to stadium and tell fans to change how they have been supporting their teams for decades. I do not use vulgar language or sing the songs but within the stadium that is what happens so if you want to come then get used to it.'* She questions why women should be seen as powerless victims who cannot hold their *own in a men's world*. This portrayal of women as victims removes the agency of female fans that chose to embrace masculine fan behaviors. Such women are seen as victims of a system that forces them to embrace masculinity to fit in and not as active agents who are actively configuring their own unique fan identities. Fandom is a relational process, which happens in interaction with others within the group. It is spatial in nature and as such the stadiums provide different context of relating along gender lines.

We are here for the football: Forget about the singing

Other women ignore vulgar language of stadiums and concentrate on the football. They believe that the abuse is not enough to keep them away from stadiums. Such type of women usually choose to sit away from where large numbers of male fans are located thus at times pay higher ticket prices to sit where there are not many people. Listening to vulgar songs is a small price to pay to watch their favorite team live. One of the research participants in this category argued that, *'I love football and I love my team so I come to the stadium despite the fact that I hate the language used by most male supporters'*. From the focus group discussions it was clear that this category of fans had accepted the state of affairs within stadiums but thought the best way to survive was to avoid the spaces where most fans sat and sing. The participants agreed that there was very little that can be done to remedy the situation as this was engrained within the football culture in Zimbabwe.

Avoidance thus forms a second major way of dealing with the phallocentric nature of stadiums. The whole football metaphor and experience is based on a heterosexual encounter in which men dominate. Being a football fan means experiencing this metaphor every time you attend matches yet women interviewed had a different opinion. They opined that football in itself has no meaning but rather society constructs sexual innuendos around the game. These symbolic constructions can be challenged, reconfigured and reconstructed as noted by one of the participants, '*vakuru vedu vebhora havazi serious nenyaya yekupedza zvinyadzi kubhora. Zvinopera izvi vakaisa mitemo plus kugadzirisa mastadium nepekugara. But chakanyanya kukosha kudzidzisa masupporter kuti zvakaipa kuti vakadzi nekuti ticharega kuuya kubhora masupporter oita mashoma*' (football leaders are letting us down. They should improve the stadiums and introduce measures that curb abuse of women. Most importantly they should promote awareness campaigns because they will lose out if women stop coming to games).

From group discussions with women in this category it showed that they were outraged by the abusive nature of the stadium but felt powerless about how to change the situation. With erratic coverage of games on television women are forced to come to stadiums if they want to watch football. Yet coming to stadiums is associated with serious problems for women. The lack of power mainly stems from what one woman called 'huge number of males versus females in stadiums. Maybe if women became the majority things will change'. Men dominate football crowds the world over and this domination reinforces the notion that stadiums are male spaces and women should stay away.

Whilst this strategy of silence and avoidance appear as if women are giving up the fight against stadium sexism, it is a potent tool of dismantling patriarchal nature of football fandom. Simply being in the stadium is potent enough to challenge stereotypes and deconstruct hegemonic ideas about a 'proper fan'. As women increase in number within the stadiums in Zimbabwe, this will ultimately impact how they respond and influence the nature of language spoken. This thesis is supported by Ben-Porat (2009) who argues that the increasing presence of women at football matches has assumed enormous significance in challenging the male hegemony over the game. Hargreaves (2000) adds that becoming female fans is metaphorically a process of conquering a piece of land in 'men's territory': the football ground has always been 'male's land'.

Stadium is not for us: women who love football but forego the stadium

The third category of fans, which I came across during this research, is women who love football and their teams but now refrain from going to the stadiums. For such women the level of misogyny is driving away many potential fans in a country were football teams desperately need as many fans as they can. In an interview with one of the fans in this category she noted that: 'We have a serious problem in this country with marketing our sports and soccer in general. Women are the majority of the population and offer a potential huge market for football teams yet very little is being done to court this market. What you get is stadiums full of vulgar and abusive language' (Focus group discussion, 14 March 2013, City Centre). Many women thus avoid stadiums and opt to follow the games via radio, on line and sometimes on television. Quitting the stadium means protesting with your money and clubs in Zimbabwe have not done anything to remedy the situation. My informal discussions with some club officials highlighted how they are not interested in improving stadium experience for women. They argued that the vulgar and abusive fans have been loyal to the league for many years and as such they cannot afford to alienate them on the promise that more female fans will come. The official noted how there are many other reasons such as finances, time and family commitments that limit the number of women fans at stadiums. There is thus very little will amongst administrators to combat misogyny within stadiums.

Staying away from games has thus done very little for women who wish to change fan cultures. What is clear is that misogynistic language has been accepted as part of football culture. It is engrained within the psyche of male fans (Chiweshe 2012: 18):

Fandom is a bastion of hegemonic masculinity. Football stadiums provide an arena in which masculinity is constructed around a clear and distinct set of defining norms. Exaltation of manhood is part of football in Zimbabwe. The songs and chants tell a story of masculine domination of an opponent which is feminised.

Women who love football are forced to suffer through in silence. Complaining is met by accusations of being 'fake fans' by male counterparts. To be accepted female fans have to accept masculine norms within stadiums. Boycotting the stadium is thus the only option for women who cannot ignore or participate in fan cultures. Women in this category also complained that being in the stadium also met with negative stereotype and stigma from other women in their communities. 'Decent' women cannot be seen at soccer stadiums unless in the company of their husbands. Thus there is also a social stigma against women who attend matches on their own without male company.

Conclusion

The discussion has provided an insight into how female football fans in Zimbabwe cope with the phallocentric and misogynistic nature of football stadiums. It highlighted three categories of female fans namely: fans who join and act like men; fans who ignore and avoid parts of the stadium with singing fans; and fans who avoid the stadiums altogether. Stadiums are socially constructed as men only spaces and as such women who venture into this territory will suffer some form of sexism whether directly or indirectly. The need to belong and be part of the group leads to many women taking up male fan behaviors and becoming 'one of the boys.' Discussions above have shown how this process of dissociation further entrenches widely held stereotypes about women and femininity. Other women were shown to favor avoidance by choosing seats within the stadium where there is less singing and thus less vulgar or foul language. Such seats tend to be in more expensive parts of the stadium but still they are not immune to abuse in these areas. Women still come to games because they love football but feel they can do little to change the status quo. The chapter also highlights women who have altogether quit the stadium. Such women see no need in being in a place where the demeaning of women is proudly practiced. They still love football but would rather follow it using radio, television, internet or newspapers. Thus the above discussion has provided an analysis to these varying coping mechanisms employed by female fans.

Chapter VI

Of Goals and Whores: Football Fandom and Misogynistic Songs at the Rufaro Stadium in Zimbabwe

Introduction

This chapter focuses on the creation and recreation of women's bodies through songs and chants among football fans in Harare. It offers an analysis of how stadiums are arenas for the celebration and reinforcement of hegemonic masculinities. Football fandom has proved a fertile ground for the display of masculine identities and the stadium has proved a readymade arena for the playing out of these identities. Fandom is a bastion of hegemonic masculinity. Football stadiums provide an arena in which masculinity is constructed around a clear and distinct set of defining norms. Exaltation of manhood is part of football in Zimbabwe. Patriarchal views on women are played out in the game of football through songs and chants. Hegemonic masculinity is performed and reinforced within the stadiums. Vulgar and misogynistic language ensures that watching football in Zimbabwe remains a male domain.

The following discussion endeavors to offer a critical analysis of the songs and chants at football matches in Zimbabwe. Such songs and chants have become an important part of football fandom and are expressions of hegemonic masculinities. The chapter offers an analysis of the creation and recreation of woman's body and its portrayal within the stadiums. It highlights that the stadium is not particularly female friendly. What happens at stadiums in countries where football has such a huge following mirrors the dominant and hegemonic ideas about social life and sexuality. In analysing the songs, chants and talk at stadiums this chapter emphasizes that the masculine nature of football fandom is one way in which sexual domination of women is celebrated and reinforced.

Football songs and chants in Zimbabwe are punctuated with many misogynistic messages, which celebrate male sexual domination. The songs degrade women and perceive sport as a sexual encounter in which the losing team is portrayed as a woman. The stadium is thus a theatre for asserting male dominance. The message to young boys attending such matches becomes clear: women are there to be used and are losers. Even young boys playing soccer on the dusty streets celebrate a goal as *hure* (whore) or a win *tavakwira* (we have sexed them). Football songs are an integral part of fandom identities as Back suggests, 'it is primarily through songs and banter that a structure of feeling is produced in football stadiums' (Back 2001: 311). Collingson (2009: 16) adds that songs are indispensable to football fans because, aside from their own massed physical presence, bedecked in team colors and the deployment of flags and banners, they have little control over the visual appearance of a stadium. The typical football fan in Zimbabwe remains black male from the working or low/poor classes. The stadium was in the past not considered a place for upright females. This chapter shows that this view persists today among soccer fans in Zimbabwe, highlighting how the football fandom recreates and reinforces the perceived inferiority of women. Young males taken to stadiums by their fathers, brothers or uncles grow up believing these sexual stereotypes. Through the analysis of songs sung by fans and direct observation of fan behaviors the chapter explores how football fandom has remained masculine and misogynistic.

Watching soccer games – especially in the stadium, as opposed to at home – is a predominantly male pursuit. Armstrong (1998), in his study of football hooliganism, found that only 10% of fans at FC United Sheffield games were female, and there is no reason to believe that this percentage would differ substantially elsewhere (certainly, the anecdotal, visual evidence of televised soccer matches indicates as much). In part, this imbalance is due to tradition, as well as the potential for violence ascribed to soccer arenas; moreover, the fact that fans will be in close and sometimes uncomfortable physical proximity - also marks them as traditionally gender-inappropriate for women. The heavily masculine nature of football teams fosters a culture of misogynistic behavior that makes young players see themselves as powerful and privileged, and anyone else – including women – as lesser objects. Women attending football matches in Zimbabwe are often victims to chants of *hure* (prostitutes).

Misogyny is most simply defined as the dislike or hate of women. Traditional feminist theorists paint many different attitudes as misogyny. According to feminists, in its most overt expression, a misogynist will openly hate all women simply because they are female. In feminist theory, other forms of misogyny may be less overt. Some alleged misogynists may simply be prejudiced against all women, or may hate women who do not fall into one or more acceptable categories. The term misogynist is frequently used in a looser sense as a term of derision to describe anyone who holds an unpopular or distasteful view about women as a group. In the same manner the nature of songs and chants at football stadiums degrade women and portray them as weaklings.

Football chants and songs: Global vulgarity

Agnew (2006) highlights the masculine nature of football fandom in an analysis of fans in Italy. Football fandom is highly gendered with the vast majority being male fans. This is mainly due to the stadium environment, which is dominated by vulgar songs that mostly denigrate women. Hesse-Lichtenberger (2006) notes how in Germany, in 2005, Borussia Dortmund fans came to the stadium, in a game against local rival Schalke, holding a large banner bearing "fuck you Schalke" and waving huge pink penises in the air. Such an atmosphere in most countries is seen as inappropriate for young females. Football fan identities are thus masculine in nature and tend to look down upon femininity. Football like other sports is about pursuing and conquering. Victors are seen as portraying male virility whilst losers are seen as portraying feminine weakness.

In England players are also abused via derogatory references to wives, girlfriends, or other female relatives, particularly if the woman concerned is famous, or if the player is known to have had an extramarital affair. The most infamous chant, 'does she take it up the arse?' was directed at David Beckham about his wife, Victoria 'Posh Spice' Beckham (Jones 2008: 521). Jones (2008) adds that sexist comments are directed at women connected with the game. For example, abuse was directed at Wendy Toms, the first and only female assistant referee in the English Premier League (She served from 1997 to 2005.) Ball girls, female stewards, female police officers, and women who come onto the pitch at half-time such as pop stars, cheerleaders, dancers, or female footballers can be subject to chants like 'get your tits out for the lads' and 'get your kit (clothes) off.' The dominant or hegemonic gender regime in soccer stadiums gives rise to sexist language that demeans women.

In 2009 the famous former coach of the Argentine football team, Diego Maradona was banned for blurting out vulgar and offensive comments after his team won. He was quoted as saying, 'To those who did not believe in us - and, ladies, forgive me - they can suck it (my penis), and keep on sucking it... You lot take it up the ass - if the ladies will pardon the expression.' Though he was fined to saying this in public such language, symbols and utterances are a normal part of football fandom worldwide. Misogynistic utterances are a normal part of being a fan at the stadium. Armstrong and Young (2008) note that ritualised football singing can exclude as well as include, as songs reflect and produce the self/other, insider/outsider binary that defines football culture. In this instance women mostly become the weakened, useless and outside 'other'. Female references are used to portray the opposition team and fans. The opposition is alluded to in sexual derogatory terms for example among by Sydney Football Club Fans in Australia goes like this, 'Your sister is your mother; your father is your brother; you all fuck one another' (Collingson 2009: 20). Karen Gosling argues that sport provides an opportunity for the 'legitimate expression of hypermasculinity' (2007: 253).

To understand misogyny and fandom this research will employ concepts of 'gender regime' or 'state of play in [the] sexual politics' of the football crowd (Connell 1987: 99). Gender has been theorised by explaining its production at the individual and structural levels through practices, interactions or performative iterations. Gender is conceived as a verb to emphasize its dynamism and potential instability (Jones 2008). For Connell (2005: 72) masculinities and femininities are 'configurations of practice.' Indeed, masculinities (and by implication femininities) are 'simultaneously a place in gender relations, the practices through which men and women engage that place in gender, and the effects of these practices in bodily experience, personality and culture' (Connell 2005: 71).

The dominant and most idealized form of masculinity in any gender regime is 'hegemonic masculinity,' a normative standard against which 'all other men ... position themselves... and [which] ideologically legitimate[s] the global subordination of women to men' (Connell 2005: 77; Connell and Messerschmidt 2005: 832). According to Demetriou (2001) hegemonic masculinity generates two kinds of hegemony: internal and external. Internal hegemony is the hierarchy of power among men, such as the relationship between the football authorities and fans. External hegemony uses hierarchies among masculinities to bolster 'the institutionalization of men's dominance over women,' thereby sustaining the current gender order (Connell and Messerschmidt 2005: 844). For instance, the homophobic feminization of gay men reinforces the social construction of femininity as negative (Kimmel 2002). Any feminine traits in players and fans alike are shunned.

Jones (2008) outlines various kinds of masculinities associated with fandom. The most common is complicit masculinities in which men practice the hegemonic masculinity but compromise with women. These men enjoy the benefits of patriarchy without overtly supporting it. This might explain why fans who do not sing along to misogynistic songs see no problem with the songs in that context and actually bring girlfriends to soccer matches. There are however more overt masculine practices consistent with 'protest' or 'oppositional' masculinities within the stadium. These are exaggeratedly aggressive or violent masculine practices carried out mostly by economically or culturally marginalised males. Engagement in these hyper masculine practices might manifest as resistance to authority among men who otherwise experience powerlessness because of their marginal positions in society (Connell 2005). Because football's fan base has diversified in terms of race, sexuality, and class, practices associated with "subordinated" or "marginalised masculinities" also occur in the stadiums (Connell 2005).

Within sport fandom patriarchy is legitimated through hegemonic masculinity, which defines gender practices such as aggression, physical strength, and competition as dominant because these practices are constructed in relation to women and subordinated masculinities (Connell 1987, 1995, 2000). Connell's (2005) framework points to the fact that people practice masculinities and femininities rather than having or being them. This means that aspects of various masculinities can exist simultaneously in the same person, so that someone can engage in protest masculinity while being respectful to women (Connell 2005). This explains why men who are respectful to women outside the stadium practice misogynistic acts at soccer matches. However, masculinities are not fixed no matter how rigid they may appear.

To understand fan behavior within the stadium, the chapter utilises Small's (1998) concept of musicking. Musicking is a musical act that 'establishes in the place where it happens a set of relationships, and it is in those relationships that the meaning of the act lies' (Small 1998: 13). Through musicking, football songs produce identity through their ritualised performance in public spaces. This performance of such secular rituals provides: 'an affirmation of community'; 'an act of exploration' [becoming]; 'an act of celebration' (Small 1998: 95). In the end singing is a marker of one's membership of a community, it produces that idealised community and it also celebrates that community, one that includes the team (Collingson 2009: 17). Thus in singing football songs people engage in affective creation of sociability and establishment of a rhetorical territory (Auge 1995: 108), 'where one is at ease in the rhetoric of the people with whom one shares a life' (Allon 2000: 285). In the case of football fans the sharing of vulgar and misogynistic songs creates a territory of hegemonic masculinity. The celebration and reinforcement of patriarchy is complete.

In a study of eight-year-old and nine-year-old South African primary school boys on masculinity and sport, Bhana (2008) notes that young boys' early association with sport is centrally about identity and doing sport, or at least establishing interest in sport is one important way in claiming to be a real boy. Young boys' developing relationship with football as fans is inscribed within particular gendered context in which everything feminine is denounced and portrayed negatively. Football fandom is replete with masculinising practices, and for many boys coming to the stadiums an image of a real man is constructed around male supremacy, physical prowess and misogynistic values. The stadium thus 'plays a key role in boys emerging masculinities and in the denigration of weak boys and girls through the constant policing of gender identities' (Bhana 2008: 11). Sport is thus a salient conduit of hegemonic masculinities and partriachial values.

Songs and language of the stadium in Zimbabwe

The language of the stadium can be understood through Bakhtin's conceptualization of language as dialogic (Lodge 1990). Language is an object of a multiple representations of the cosmology of the users of that language. The dominant ideologies of any system are transmitted and practiced through language. Patriarchy thus uses language as a powerful tool to entrench women's subordination. In this study language of the stadium is thus a representation of the dominant patriarchal views on women. Through this language, stereotypes about women are passed from older men to young boys. Football songs are a form of language that conveys meaning not only about the game but a society's culture in general.

Fans use songs to motivate their players by praising their masculinity as a way of increasing their performance levels. Many such songs portray the maleness and virility of the team for example Dynamos fans have the following song *'DeMbare yaita mamonya'* (Dynamos have strong men). Note that the reinforcement of strength and maleness in the song. The word *monya* means a muscular and well-built man who is able to beat up others. Physicality is part of being male and aggression is part of performing this masculine persona. This *monya* persona is the ultimate representation of hegemonic masculinity as it portrays the machismo associated with men in Zimbabwe. Yet other songs use symbolise the team as an unstoppable force for example, *'Dembare moto, dembare moto unopisa'* (Dynamos is like a fire which burns) or *'hona kepe, kepe kepe bhora'* (Caps United are football). There are songs used to increase morale among the fans such 'Daira supporter, *daira* supporter, *kudaira ndadaira, daira* supporter' (Sing supporter, sing) or to chide fans who are not singing, *'asiri kuimba pamhata'* (if you are not singing, you are an asshole). The feeling is that a real fan comes to the stadium to be part of the singing and not just to watch the game. To affirm your fan credentials, one has to engage in the singing. Engaging in the singings reaffirms the dominant believes and stereotypes of male superiority. These stereotypes represent the ideologies of wider society. These songs however celebrate male virility and thereby uphold hegemonic views of what real man ought to be.

The portrayal of the opposition always mostly is in sexual terms. The opposition team is seen as weak women who are there to lose. The language before games among fans reverberates around *'tinovaisa or tinovakwira'* (we will fuck them). These songs can be very nasty and very graphic for example *'Team yemadhodhi Kepekepe'* (Caps are full of shit) or *'Honde iya hondende kateam kaye kamama'* (that small team has been fucked). The sexual connotations are a theme that runs through the songs as shown by another song that had the words, *'Highlanders taikwira kuseniseni'* (we have fucked Gunners early in the game). At a Caps United game, an old man stood up when a rival player was tackled to the ground and shouted, *'Mame mame mame, mamama'* (you have been fucked). Within the stadium competition between two teams becomes a sexual contest in which the loser is labelled a woman. Rival supporters view opponents as vaginas, which they will ultimately enter. Scoring a goal and winning is then viewed as sexual contest.

The celebration of hegemonic masculinity is the hallmark of stadium behavior. Connell's (2005) conceptualization of hegemonic masculinities illuminates the inherent gender slurs in stadium language. Some of the songs are targeted at rival players and coaches. One example is a song sang by Dynamos fans that went as follows, *'Tsipa iwewe, hahaahaaa, Tsipa iwewe, wakauya wega kuzorohwa nyoro'* (Tsipa (Caps United player) you came on your own will to get fucked). Caps United fans replied by mocking the Dynamos coach saying, *'Chuchu wabe-cheya, matadza madzamai dai mamurova gumbo-ro'* (Chuchu was the Dynamos coach at the time of research). The song simply means he stole a chair and should be beaten but emphasis is on the words *wa[be-che]ya* which might mean vagina and *gu[mboro]* meaning penis).

All the songs that I came across that were meant to chide opposition fans were riddled with vulgar words and messages. The sexual and graphic nature of the songs was clear and the stadium environment made it possible for such social taboos to be played out. Another interesting song that highlighted how social issues and nicknames of players interrelate goes as, '*Makanaka ndiye ega anorohwa nyoro, baba mumufongorese*' (Makanaka is the only who is fucked without a condom). Makanaka is a young television personality in Zimbabwe who was impregnated before she turned sixteen. However, one of Caps United's young players is nicknamed Makanaka because of his young age and in reference to the television personality. The song speaks to the pregnancy of the television personality and the Caps United player at the same time. The young girl portrayed in a negative way as a sex object. Various incidences of violence are performed on the female body within the stadium. In the name of fandom women are abused, degraded and portrayed as inferior beings. Another song has the words, '*Boziwero chave chimanje manje, boziwero kana nechembere kwira*' (Rich man times have changed, nowadays you can have sex with very old people).

These songs appear to be in the majority of songs collected in this research. Again the sexual and graphic nature of the songs is telling. Other songs have hidden innuendos so much that they can become popular even to those who do not attend football matches without realising the true meaning. An example is when Zimbabwe qualified for the Africa Nations Cup in 2004 the song '*Ndiri kuvaviwa mai mwana, ndikwenyeiwo*' (I have an itch, my wife please help me) became popular nationally. The problem is that the itch had sexual innuendos in that the itch was about being horny and the wife was supposed to provide the required help. Another song contains the words, '*Tete here, handina ukama nemi ikamira ndoisa*' (this one relates to the aunt of the wife who is being warned that since they are not related she can be slept with). Another favorite song among fans goes as follows, '*Anna akarumwa nembwa beche rese*' (Anna's vagina was beaten off by a dog). This song makes little sense except to only make reference to a woman's vagina. Most of these types of songs are sexual in nature and misogynistic. They portray women's bodies in a sexual and negative manner.

Other songs are sexual in nature but are social commentaries such as, '*Mese muri mahure panyika pano hapana asingade nyoro here*' (you are all prostitutes because everyone in this world loves sex without a condom). Another similar song goes as '*Handina mwana anoda beche musatanyoko*' (I do not want children who love sex/vagina). This song though vulgar is a declaration by a parent that their child should not be promiscuous. Other songs are just vulgar without meaning much such as '*Amai Mariah musatanyoko, matirakidza beche tawonerera*' (Mariah's mother is an idiot, she showed us her vagina). Another song warns about the dangers of having unprotected sex but in an expletive manner. The song says, '*Kana uri wanga usarova nyoro, nyoro ndeye mhene, mhene vana Chiyangwa*' (if you are poor do not have sex without a condom that is only for the rich like Chiyangwa (Zimbabwean businessman). Other fans sing to mock the police by saying, '*Mboro yenyu officer*' (your penis officer). Gender slurs punctuate most songs for example a song goes as, '*Fongo, fongo kufongora pese pese, hakanyare, baba kachakwirwa*' (this young girl who is strutting all over the place will be fucked).

There is however songs that do not contain any vulgar words that are sang to spice up the stadium. Such songs are not surprisingly in the minority but still talk about everyday relationships. *'Emma, Emma iwe, Emma, anongondi shainira Emma, ndichangomusiyaso Emma'* (Emma is pompous so I will leave hinm alone). Another good example of such songs says *'Mukorokoza ari kuchema mugodhi wadhirika, ari kuchema mari'* (the gold panner is crying because the mine has fallen in). Some of the songs portray everyday social issues such as marital problems like in the song that sings *'Mai mwana ndozvasingade mumba mangu (he ndozvasingade mumbamangu), Tora tumapoto(tora) tumaradio (tora)'* (My wife I do not want this kind of behavior in my house, better you leave with all the pots and radios). Songs are an integral part of stadium culture however the nature of songs needs to be understood and how they influence or are influenced by the dominant ideas in society. The songs documented above are a sample of songs used by fans but they offer a perfect sample of what is sang at stadiums around Zimbabwe.

Symbols, chants, language and behaviors of stadium

Symbols and chants have an important role in identifying a team as peculiar from its competitors. The language of soccer fans is at best crude and unadulterated. Fans use vulgar idioms in every conversation for example, when calling a friend who is nearby it is common to hear, *'iwe mhata iwe'* (hey you asshole). Such language is commonplace and children who come to games grow up cultured in such stadium language. In cases where a man enters the terraces with a female companion, it is common for fans to shout *'Azvibatira ganga rake'* (he has got himself a whore). At one of the games a guy came with two big women and as he left the terraces he placed his hands when on the women's buttock whilst shouting *'Tauyanadzo tsapo dzemhata'* (We brought big pack of asses). Another occasion is when groups of fans spontaneously started shouting *'hure'* when a woman dressed in jeans or tight fitting clothes pass by.

The language of the stadium is highly sexual and graphic. It often relates to widely held views about sex and women among men. For instance fans often refer rival teams as *'mainini'* (wife's young sister). The word in this sense has sexual connotations as one fan pointed that *'mainini'* is someone you are used to have sex with and they are always available. A rival team in this sense becomes available to be sexed every time. Losing and having sex become synonymous. Sex is viewed as an act in which the women lose and men gain. At the time of the research the soccer fans had a popular saying whenever one of their players did something spectacular. They would shout, *'hona mwana wako'* (look at your child). Again this statement had sexual origins that are not apparent to the uninitiated. At that time most fans were sharing through email and cellular phones a video of two baboons having sex whilst a baby baboon was watching. The male baboon then says to the female *'hona mwana wako'* (look at your child). This story highlights how things with sexual innuendos ultimately gain popularity among soccer fans.

Abuse is hailed at players who are seen as not giving enough effort. It is very common to hear things such as, *'ari kutamba kunge mukadzi'* (he is playing like a woman) or *'anongodona kunge hure'* (he is always falling down like a prostitute). These derogatory terms suggest that players are lesser men because they resemble women. They imply that being like a woman at football is to lack skill, coordination, ability, courage, and strength. The language associated with the stadium is punctuated by imagery of women as weaklings. Patriarchal views of manhood dominate football fandom as the game has been seen as a male domain for so long. Women who attend matches have so suffer through verbal and in some circumstances physical abuse.

In all the matches attended there were very few posters or placards borne by supporters. The few posters did not carry any sexual or misogynistic messages. The majority of supporters carried flags with them that had team colors and logos. Another interesting aspect was celebrations when a goal was scored. The vast majority of fans would jump up shouting '*hure*' (whore). From street games to national league, a goal is greeted with the shout of '*hure*' (whore). Most fans I came across did not know how this association came about but all gave a sexual explanation of what it possibly means. One fan in particular indicated that scoring a goal was like entering a woman and for him the ecstasy was similar thus the first thing that comes to his mind after a goal is a woman. Another fan gave another view on the matter noting that '*hure*' was a way of mocking the opposition who had finally surrendered like a woman opening her legs for a man to enter.

Discussion

Following, Armstrong and Young (2008) the ritualised singing at Rufaro stadium exclude and include, as songs reflect and produce the self/other, insider/outsider binary that defines football culture. Women are made to feel as objectified others that do not belong. Sex becomes a symbol of strength, virility and prowess. Losers are portrayed as women and unmanly. The virtues of manhood are glorified and young fans grow up trying to live out this portrayal of masculinity. The stadium is a male cauldron where females enter at their own peril. Phallic symbols punctuate everything about football fandom in Zimbabwe. Soccer fandom is traditionally a patriarchal institution that effectively serves the reproduction of hegemonic masculinity and allows little room for women, because femininity is constructed as an object of sexual conquest and physical inferiority. From the description of scoring as a sexual act to losing team being likened to women (women's vagina more precisely), sexist symbols are part and parcel of fandom.

Through musicking (Small 1998: 13) fans create and recreate masculine relationships and misogyny. Stadium language only makes meaning in its location that is why the same language is not spoken at home. Football matches are places were hegemonic masculine traits practiced in society perversely through patriarchy are openly celebrated and reinforced. Whilst the singing happens within the context of the stadiums, the beliefs about women's inferiority are part of everyday life in Zimbabwe. The men carry these attitudes with them wherever they are. The stadium offers them a context to celebrate what they are already practicing in their lives. Sport can be especially powerful in the reproduction of patriarchal gender relations because it is a cultural site where social notions of masculinity based on a belief in men's physical superiority over women can be recreated (Connell 1987).

Fandom is a bastion of hegemonic masculinity. Football stadiums provide an arena in which masculinity is constructed around a clear and distinct set of defining norms. Exaltation of manhood is part of football in Zimbabwe. The songs and chants tell a story of masculine domination of an opponent which is feminised. Feminisation of opposing teams is a vital part of watching and supporting football. The dominant gender regime in football thus remains highly masculine. Fandom promotes an orthodox form of masculinity that promotes socio negative (sexist, misogynistic, and anti-feminine) attitudes toward women. Anderson (2008) notes that as a highly segregated, homophobic, sexist, and misogynistic gender regime, sport fandom not only contribute to the gender order, but it also reproduce a conservative and stabilising form of masculinity.

Conclusion

Stadium is an arena of celebrating hegemonic masculinities. It offers a ready-made environment in which virtues of maleness and virility are openly upheld. Football songs, chants and language are misogynistic and full of sexual innuendos. Celebration of masculine values is part of being a fan. Patriarchal views on women are played out in the game of football through songs and chants. Hegemonic masculinity is performed and reinforced within the stadiums. Vulgar and misogynistic language ensures that watching football in Zimbabwe remains a male domain. In conclusion football in Zimbabwe will remain a male domain as long as the fans are allowed to use abusive languages. Phallocentric songs and symbols of male domination discourage women from attending football matches yet gate takings are the biggest sources of revenue for football teams in Zimbabwe. A gender sensitive environment will attract more spectators and consequently added revenue.

Chapter VII

Creation and Meaning of Symbols among Dynamos Football Club Fans in Zimbabwe

Introduction

Football remains the most popular sport in Zimbabwe. This chapter provides an analysis of the creation of symbols associated with teams such as nicknames, colours and rituals. It argues that in Zimbabwe the creation of symbols is a contested enterprise and even the names of some team are contested. Football transcends the realm of the physical and attains a spiritual importance for most fans within the African continent. Supporting a football team goes beyond the ninety minutes of game time and the stadium. Football teams become the extension of the self and as such fans feel they are part and parcel of the teams they support. Fans are thus fundamental members of the football teams and as such are involved in the creation and recreation of symbols associated with these teams. The chapter offers an analysis into the meaning and importance of such symbols. Theory of symbolic interactionism facilitates understanding of the negotiation and contestations that exist in symbol creation and in understanding the meanings of such symbols.

This chapter offers a nuanced analysis of how football fans are involved in the creation and meaning of symbols associated with their teams using supporters of Dynamos Football Club in Zimbabwe as a case study. The main focus of this chapter is to offer a grounded analysis on how fans are involved in the enterprise of meaning creation at football teams in an African context. Football fandom offers the chance for individuals to display their identities as part of something that is bigger than them. In such an enterprise the team is not something foreign or outside the individual rather it is part and parcel of their existence and in some ways defines them as a person. Sport teams have a lot of symbols associated to them that include flags, home grounds, chants/slogans, badges, nicknames, colours and many other items, which mean something to the fans and the teams. This can include certain pre and post-match team rituals, which are performed to distinguish the team from its competitors. The assumption of this chapter is that the creation, recreation and meaning of such symbols is a contested enterprise. It will prove this by looking and the fans of Dynamos Football Club fans in Zimbabwe.

The chapter highlights that different symbols mean different things to different supporters depending on such variables as age. It will highlight that the creation of such symbols is not a straightforward process but rather one that is full of contestations and even the source of the name of the team is contested. Borrowing from the symbolic interactionist school the chapter illustrates that as fans interact; meanings are created, contested and reproduced. Emotional investment in a team leads to fans personalising and internalising the team as part of their person. As such symbols associated with teams become extensions of individuals and thus hold much currency for fans. Team symbols are collectively shared and thus become a rallying point and a physical identifier of one's allegiance. According to Firth (1973: 74-75) a symbol represents a condensed and coded significance, 'a complex series of associations, often of an emotional kind' which otherwise is inconvenient and difficult to explain or describe (Firth 1973: 74-75).

This definition highlights the representative nature of a symbol. Football fandom is often, to borrow from Firth (1973: 74-75) 'a complex series of associations, usually of an emotional nature'. It is difficult to explain or describe the love of a fan for a team. Symbols help in signifying this love through associating it to visible or tangible things such as flags or emblems. Edler and Cobb (1983: 28) argue an object becomes a symbol when people endow it with meaning, value or significance and without this it remains an object. Symbols are thus subjective and context specific that means that they only make sense to certain people in specific contexts. Through language and communication, symbols provide the means by which reality is constructed. Individuals and groups interact based on meanings drawn from prevailing symbols. In the same way football fans interact with each other according to shared meanings that are specific to that group. Fans, based on repeated interaction share stadium language, symbols and meaning.

Symbolic interactionism and the creation of meaning

The symbolic aspect of team colours, history and songs can be important in how fans view themselves. Blumer (1969) argues that symbols are one of the most important aspects of symbolic interactionism. He highlights that symbolic interactionism has its three basic premises: (1) Humans act toward things on the basis of the meanings that things have for them; (2) the meanings of things derive from social interaction; and (3) these meanings are dependent on, and modified by, an interpretive process of the people who interact with one another (Blumer 1969). The meaning of a thing resides in the action that it elicits. For example, the meaning of 'team colors' is multiple and diverse. In the case of symbols, meanings also depend on a degree of consensual responses between different fans. While the social world is composed of material and objective features, what distinguishes humans is their extensive and creative use of communication through symbols. The history, culture, and forms of communication of humans can be traced through symbols and it is through symbols that meaning is associated with interpretation, action, and interaction.

At one level symbols may seem fixed, but the symbolic interaction perspective emphasizes the shifting, flexible, and creative manner in which humans use symbols. It is thus through the use of symbols that are associated with certain sporting teams that the fan starts to make sense of his/her world as he/she creates meaning of his/her existence. People arbitrarily construct symbols and they become short cuts to meaning, used again and again (Society for More Creative Speech (SMCS) 1996).

Since all meaning is subjective analysis of any given behaviour will vary by group. Symbolic interactionists researching different groups may come to different conclusions about the same behaviour because symbols and their meanings vary by group. Even within a group various individuals have different meanings for the same symbols. Prus (1995) argues that symbols have temporal and spatial variations thus they are not constant over groups, generations or geography. In terms of football fandom the symbols and meanings of teams among fans is therefore affected by their age, gender, where they live and in some cases class. In most instances the meaning of symbols is created through experience within a group thus it is through interaction with other fans that most individuals place meanings to symbols associated with their teams of choice.

Using Goffman's (1958) dramaturgy the behaviour of fans can be seen as role taking. The stadium acts as a theatre in which fan behaviours are scripted but can be improvised by the actors. The fans' behave in the expected manner as they cheer and sing for their teams in their regalia. They are hostile to the opposing team and its supporters. Being a fan thus requires one to play the part. This explains why most fans at stadiums act in ways they do not normally do within their everyday lives such as singing the often-vulgar songs. The symbols which include elaborate costumes made of team colours, face and body paintings, flags, scarves, specially made hats, blowing horns, bells, drums and other associated regalia are part of the act and enhance the performance of the role of being a fan. Symbols in this instance can be seen a means of playing out fan roles and only make sense within the context of fandom.

Through language and communication, symbols provide the means by which reality is constructed. Individuals and groups interact based on meanings drawn from prevailing symbols. Symbols do not have meaning in themselves; humans attach meaning to them. For example, the colours worn by a sporting team can have a significant meaning to fans that support that team. The self-concept is essentially the product of social interaction. Symbols and their meanings thus are negotiated in social interaction to an extent that a symbol can have different meaning to different people. Symbolic interactionism helps understand the negotiated and contested nature of symbols within groups. Symbols of sporting teams thus carry different and contested meanings to the different supporters. The self is inescapably a social self. People create their identities based on the influence of others; parental and peer influences are of paramount importance.

Symbols and metaphors used to describe the team

The symbols associated with the team did not vary much by age though they certainly meant different things to the respondents. The major difference between the two age groups (Group 1 those forty years and above and Group 2 those below forty) was mainly in the source of the name Dynamos. Whilst those in Group 1 were mostly unanimous that the name was inspired by a Russian team called Dynamo Kiev. However some of the respondents in this group disagreed, one claims that the name was an original idea of the founder members thus was not inspired by another team. The source of the name was contested among the respondents though as shown in Chapter 2 on the history of Dynamos, the name was actually inspired by the Russian team Dynamo Kiev. In Group 2 however there were many explanations of the source of the name. One respondent claimed that the name was introduced to describe the dynamic nature of the team. For another respondent the name was derived from the word dynamo and another respondent it was from the word dynamite. The name itself has become a strong symbol to be associated with by the respondents but there are contestations over the source of the name. As a symbol, all supporters who might not have any knowledge about how the name was adopted or what it means share the name. Most respondents in both groups were not sure about the meaning of the name but as one young man noted, '*Kuti Dynamos, ndokuti bhora*' (Dynamos is football).

Respondents gave a lot of variations to the name that included names such as *Denamo (di-na-mo), Dile Dile (di-le di-le)*.

Madhina dhina (ma-di-na-di-na) and ultimately DeMbare. Fans from the original name of the team created all these variations. This shows how fans are involved in the creation and production of symbols associated with teams. Fans are not passive but active members of sporting teams. Whilst the official name remains, it is interpreted and used in different ways by fans in different contexts. For example individual fans can create their own names that have no meaning to the rest of the fans. One fan actually referred to the team as *Dynamos DeCyclone*. DeCyclone is a word created from combining the prefix de- to the word cyclone. Most names created by fans start with this prefix, which is an important aspect of the team. Individuals define their own unique experience and attachment to the club can thus create symbols. At times they can be shared with friends and other fans but they mostly remain individual. There are however names, which have become synonymous with the team and are shared by all fans though there are contestations over their source and meaning. One such name is Dynamos *DeMbare*.

DeMbare is the nickname widely used by the respondents in both groups to call the team. However the difference comes in that those in Group 1 (forty years and older) use the nickname Glamour Boys more often than those in Group 2 (below forty years old). This maybe because the time when Dynamos was most glamorous was when the Group 1 respondents were younger and the Group 2 supporters are hesitant to use the name which is slowly dying. Research respondents claimed that *DeMbare* literally means 'from Mbare'. One respondent informed me that the name came about when a Mauritian team which had the phrase, de Firma' (from Firma) as part of its name came to the country and beat a rival team. However this is contested as another supporter claimed that it was a Ugandan team. It was from there that the name *DeMbare* was acquired mainly because most of the players lived in Mbare, the support base was also strong in Mbare and the home ground of the team was is in Mbare. A respondent in the focus group discussions noted that it was not because most of the players or supporters came from Mbare that the name *DeMbare* came about but because it was formed in Mbare. History of names and nicknames is thus a contested territory and fans have different perceptions about the source and meaning of these names.

In the focus group discussions it was argued that it was Charles Mabika, a radio football commentator who had christened the club *DeMbare*. Other respondents who claimed that it was a certain faction of the fans that had come up with the name however disputed this. Thus though the various respondents acknowledge the nickname its source and meaning are contested. From the focus group discussions in Group 1 it could be determined that the name Glamour Boys, which was associated with the team, came mainly from the style of play, the success and the huge support for the team. One respondent claimed that there was a time when it was every players dream to play for Dynamos since it had all the glamour. Another respondent in Group 1 claimed that it was the Glamour Boys because it was the first team to sell a player to a foreign team, who was Freddy Mkwesha, to a team in Portugal called Sporting de Brugge. However for most respondents in Group 2 the name is no longer that relevant hence they are more comfortable with *DeMbare*. Another respondent claimed that it's now rare to even hear the team being referred to as the Glamour Boys on radio or in the papers. Nicknames are generational and can change with time. They have specific contextual meaning of the fans of different eras. Thus when analysing symbols and meaning associated with sports teams it is important to note that they are fluid in spatial and temporal dimensions. As generations of fans change, move and interact; there are constant shifts in team symbols and what they mean.

Due to its popularity, most respondents described the team as the team of the nation. One respondent actually called it 'de seven million'. The respondent claimed that there was a time in the 1990s when the Zimbabwean population was around seven million and it was thus claimed that all the people in the country supported the team thus it was '*de-seven million*'. The informants indicated that the argument was that everyone was a supporter of Dynamos first then the other teams because the team was synonymous with football in the country. One respondent went on to note that Dynamos did not discriminate against any ethnic group and has widespread support throughout the nation hence for him it is the team of the nation. He even went further to term Dynamos fans as *Dembabweans* (joining the word *DeMbare* and Zimbabwean). Some respondents who had grown up in the rural areas came from as diverse places as Plumtree, Chiredzi, Mt Dawin, Mhangura and Mutare. In this case there is agreement amongst fans who all agree to the wide popularity of their team. There is no study that has been done to prove whether this team really has the highest number of fans countrywide. What is certain is that the team has a huge following at stadiums across the country. Fans tend to bask in this popularity and this reflects in the pride they exhibit when talking about the team.

Another popular symbolic phrase amongst respondents in Group 1 is that, '*Dynamos haina ngozi*' (Dynamos has no bad spirits). One respondent alluded to the notion that it meant that the team was not one man's property, thus it would not be liable to the action of any man. Thus for the respondent it meant that the team belonged to everyone and it had no one recognized owner thus one could be thrown out easily if they did wrong. To show the contestations in the creation and meaning of symbols another respondent had another meaning and source of the phrase. He said that the phrase came about when a player from a team called Black Aces died on the pitch playing Dynamos. In Shona we have the '*kuchekeresa*' concept by which a human life is offered as a sacrifice for one to be successful. The Black Aces fans thought that Dynamos had done that but in response, Dynamos fans retorted '*hatina ngozi*' (our team is not bedeviled by the spirit of retribution). Though a group may share meanings and symbols, the contestation about their source and true meaning are always present and are negotiated in-group interaction. Individuals hold personal views on certain issues with regards to the club and these are mainly formed in interaction with other fans at games and bars. Asked on the source of their knowledge most respondents indicated that it was through fellow fans or older people (fathers or brothers mainly) who introduced them to Dynamos.

The respondents in the two groups indicated that the colour blue is the main symbol of the team. Though none of the respondents were sure of why the team chose the colour blue, they mostly agreed that it symbolized the blue sky. For one respondent Dynamos owned the skies and just like the sky it covered the whole world. This highlights how fans believe against all reality that their team is the best ever in the world. For a team playing in a small nation such as Zimbabwe world fame is a mere dream but for the fans their team means the world to them. To show the significance of the colour blue, another respondent cited a famous saying among the Dynamos fans that says that, "if God hated Dynamos, He would not have made the sky blue." Another respondent claimed that after becoming a fan, blue became his favourite colour and that everything he wears has to have blue in it. For another respondent the curtains, blankets, cups, plates and tablecloths at his house are all blue. For yet another respondent the colour blue represents beauty and serenity much like the style of play Dynamos has. The colour blue thus is on flags, scarves, replica jerseys, and wrist and headbands. If you are wearing blue on a match day it is synonymous with being a Dynamos supporter.

In terms of flags the Dynamos supporters come to games with flags, which are blue and white in club, with the club badge and many different messages. Among some of the messages is a saying that 'if God hated Dynamos why did he make the sky blue'. One fan indicated had a flag made out of both the Zimbabwean and Dynamos flags to show his support for the country and team. He explained this by saying for him Dynamos was Zimbabwe and Zimbabwe was Dynamos. Another flag has the message borrowed from the Liverpool fans in England which says that, 'you will never walk alone' whilst another says, 'thou shall never say die'. All these messages are written up by fans to portray what they feel or think about the club. The fans find a free avenue to express their emotions, identity and feelings. The flags are contested in the messages they portray which are highly individual. Fans use messages that portray how they see the team and what being a fan means to them.

With regards to the team logo the research informants were not able to aptly explain how and why it got into existence. The logo has a lion holding a mantle and the team's nickname (Glamour Boys) and the year they were formed (1963). The late Sam Dauya, who is credited as the club founder is said to have been responsible for designing the club's first constitution and logo. For the fans the meaning of the logo varies with how they view the symbol of the lion. Some informants highlighted that the team was the king of the Zimbabwean football in the same manner the lion is a king of the jungle. Another interesting twist was one older respondent (over forty years old) who argued that the lion represented the fact that many of the founding players were of the lion totem something that the researcher could not verify. Younger informants highlighted that the logo might have been influenced by logos from other countries just as the name Dynamos. Its significance and history is contested amongst fans that have different ways of interpreting the logo. Fans associate with these symbols and they become an expression of their loyalty and love for the team. They individualize shared symbols and create their own meanings.

Creation, recreation and meaning of symbols: a contested enterprise

For symbolic interactionist symbols like everything else are a negotiated enterprise (SMCS 1996). For the fan symbols represent something important and allow the fans to be part of something bigger than themselves. The symbols attain a consecrated place in the mundane and profane existence of fans. It is fascinating, even though sometimes frightening, how a football team gains vast and complex social signification and symbolism that overtake the simple outcome of a sporting competition. Symbolic pride is tied to support and football is therefore frequently made into 'a matter of honour'. Symbols only make sense in the environment in which they are used.

The stadium is governed by its own social rules, which are different from those of the wider community.

Symbols do not have meaning in themselves; humans attach meaning to them. For example the colour blue, which is the colour of Dynamos' uniform, has so many meanings to the respondents. The colour blue in itself means nothing but it holds many meaning for Dynamos fans. The process by which a colour attains symbolic currency is interesting in that it is context specific. The colour blue without Dynamos does not mean much for the fans but add their supporter for a team that wears that colour then everything attains a whole new meaning. The most important thing to note is that these meanings are diverse and are not agreed upon thus the colour means different things to the diverse respondents. Fans themselves usually create these meanings. It is not known why the team chose those colours and if the founding players were to be asked there will be many differing reasons for that.

The history of Dynamos is as contested as the source of the name among the respondents. The respondents in both groups did not agree on the meaning and source of the name, some claiming it was meant to mean the dynamic nature of the team, while others said the name was taken from a Russian team Dynamo Kiev. The contestation on the source of the name shows how a group of people can be brought together by something such as football teams yet not agree on many aspects of that thing. Symbolic interactionism alerts us to these contestations in the creation of social reality. Unlike with well-established teams in Europe whose histories are documented nothing about Dynamos has been documented except for the newspaper reports. The lack of official records on the history of the club allow for many differing and competing views of how it was formed.

Another important distinction between the two groups is on the nickname of the club. Whilst respondents in Group 1 mainly used the nickname Glamour Boys, respondents in Group 2 were comfortable with *DeMbare*. The older respondents in Group 1 were more nostalgic about the glorious past of the team and the times when it was christened the Glamour Boys. The respondents in Group 2 were reluctant to use this nickname given the recent past of failure, thus preferred to use *DeMbare*. This difference between the two generations of fans highlights how age can affect the importance of a symbol. The source of this nickname is also contested, though there is agreement that it means "from Mbare." Stories range from the notion that it was formed and based in Mbare, thus the name. However others disagree noting that it was inherited from a team from another African country, whilst others claimed a soccer commentator, Charles Mabika, christened it. Again the contested nature of social reality is brought to the fore by the different sources given for the name.

The nickname Glamour Boys has stood the taste of time though younger fans were now uncomfortable to use it. As noted by Paul Doyle writing for the Guardian newspaper in Britain had this to say about the Glamour Boys nickname, "Everything is relative. In Zimbabwe, Dynamos FC are nicknamed the Glamour Boys because they're the country's most popular club. But in the wider world of African, let alone global, football, that sobriquet could easily be seen as sarcastic. For financially Dynamos are in dire straits even though they can sell out their 45,000-capacity stadium" (Doyle 2008). Symbols tend to have a lasting power even when conditions do change and their meaning becomes questioned. In some instances there seems to be a recreation of the meaning of a symbol. In terms of the nickname Glamour Boys for some respondents it is still relevant because just being Dynamos is glamorous because of its success. They do not define or associate glamour with things such as money or huge salaries for players but rather with past successes. Following Goffman's (1958) thesis on dramurtagy, Dynamos fans view their roles as an important part of the club's fabric. Through carefully choreographed symbols fans became part of the performance at football matches. Symbols such as flags, colours and regalia are part of this performance.

Zora (spread) butter phenomenon

In 2011 Dynamos players and fans created phenomenon through a celebration move they performed after scoring and winning games. The celebration move is called *zora* (spread) butter. Robson Sharuko, editor of The Herald described it as: Left arm outstretched, right arm being swung from an angle into contact with the left, then the move, as if the right arm is applying something, like a lotion or butter, on the left, from the finger tips right down to the shoulder. The dance move was started by popular musician Alick Macheso at his shows and later borrowed by footballers. Players and fans symbolising unity of purpose perform the dance in unison. Celebration captured the imagination of the country beyond football fans and became synonymous with Dynamos. There is however contestations on how the dance adapted to football. Tapiwa Kapini, Zimbabwe national team goalkeeper was probably the first player to do the dance yet Dynamos supporters I came across claim that it was their team who started with the dance. Some football symbols are borrowed and adopted from popular arts and everyday practices but they gain symbolic currency when they associated with sports institutions.

Rufaro Stadium: Spiritual home for Dynamos fans

The stadium is an important symbol for Dynamos fans because it is the only physical artefact that relates to their team. Dynamos do not have offices or headquarters thus Rufaro Stadium takes an important symbolic meaning. From the first sight of the 'green' of the pitch, the smell of the terraces, to the sense of history and tradition that are a part of bricks and mortar of the ground, being there is highly emotive (Social Issues Research Centre 2008). One old fan in Group One had this to say: "Rufaro Stadium is our spiritual home. It is a symbol of who we are as a team especially the fact that it is located in Mbare. When we are in the stadium we feel at home. We will forever be identified by Rufaro Stadium even though over the years we have at times lost access to the stadium as it is owned by council." Another young fan in Group Two: "Rufaro Stadium is much more than a stadium in which the games are played but a cathedral to practice our own type of religion because Dynamos is a religion." Experiencing life in the stadium and the passions evoked by it serves to reinforce fans' sense of belonging to their club. Many fans felt that Rufaro is hallowed ground and represents a place of love and acceptance for them.

Conclusion

Symbols remain an integral part of fandom as they form an intrinsic part of how fans celebrate their identities. The preceding discussion has highlighted how the creation of symbols associated with sporting teams is a contested enterprise. It argued that such symbols only make sense in specific contexts and that they define how particular individuals relate to the teams they support. Football fandom is associated with footballing vestiges, which are historical reminders of where the club has come from and provide meaning for such clubs. Symbols are thus a celebration of fandom and allow fans to provide a physical outlet to deeper emotional feelings of attachment that are otherwise difficult to express. The chapter has used the theory of symbolic interactionism to highlight how the creation and meaning of symbols among sports fans are negotiated and contested. Drawing on theorists such as Blumer (1969) and Goffman (1958) the discussion highlighted how symbols are subjective and hold a special meaning for those who part of a group.

Chapter VIII

Cyber-Fandoms in Zimbabwe

Introduction

Using netnography, this chapter explores presentation and contestation of fan identities on Facebook. The virtual nature of these fan identities is part of entrenched nature of our increasingly bifurcated society. People have fandoms practiced in the realm of cyber and real life. The chapter outlines actual conditions, motivation, symbolic meaning, and performance of online fan identities. It questions how the emergence of new media has mediated establishment and performative practices of football fandoms. Our study concludes that we are witnessing a new form of fandom, one based not on physical but on virtual geography, in which fan identities can be exported and practiced thousands of miles away from the team and other fans and in which consumption of football is mediated via fan forums.

This is the era of 'clickfans' who 'like,' 'comment,' and 'post.' Online discussions, complaints, debates, and chats allow fan interaction even with football players and sports journalists who are also on Facebook. Social media thus mediates a fandom that allows more interaction amongst fans but less physical contact. The chapter shows how online behaviors of fans in Zimbabwe highlight how fundamentally social media has increased the degree of self-consciousness and reflexivity to football fans' performances of their fandom.

The popularity of Facebook continues to grow exponentially in Zimbabwe. With the rise of mobile internet access and the increase of cheap smartphones on the market many urban and even rural people are fast becoming netzens. Facebook offers a platform for instant communication and meeting of people in different spaces. Many Zimbabweans are spending hours a day at local internet cafes to keep up to date with their Facebook page or to stay in touch with friends and family. Mzaca (2012) argues that in Zimbabwe, Facebook is as popular and essential as water. It has become so important that people cannot imagine life before Facebook era. The study targeted the Facebook sites of Zimbabwean football clubs.

Table 8.1 provides details of number of supporters visiting each of those sites. These Facebook pages were purposively chosen on the basis of the numbers of followers. There are many fan platforms for the three sampled teams, which is one interesting feature about Facebook. The pages were all started and are managed by fans. Any fan with access to the internet can start a fan page but there are only a few that have gained popularity to the extent that they are attracting thousands of followers. It is these sites where a wide range of fans meet, network and interact that are the center of this analysis. Purposively sampling of these fan pages allows an exploratory enterprise into online fandoms within an African context. As such, Facebook, because of its popularity in Zimbabwe, offered the best option to provide insights into how social media is influencing fan identities.

Table 8.1: Team Facebook Site Followers

Team	Site	Followers
Highlanders FC	http://www.facebook.com/Amahlolanyama?fref+ts	15,087
Caps United FC	http://www.facebook.com/realCupKings?fref=ts	10,040
Caps United FC	http://www.facebook.com/kepekepebhora?fref=ts	6,887
Dynamos FC	http://www.facebook.com/grous/dynamosfc.dembare/?fref=ts	8,771
Dynamos FC	http://www.facebook.com/va.shagare?fref=ts	82,187

The importance of football in the everyday lives of its fans cannot be overemphasized. Chiweshe (2016), using Dynamos Football Club fans in Zimbabwe, demonstrates the nexus between social identity and supporting a football club. Alegi (2010) notes how by 1960, football was an established component of African urban culture. Africans have learned, adopted, and achieved a noticeable cultural appropriation of the game across the continent. Zimbabwean football is a colonial construct. The Pioneer Column's men were the first players of football and rugby (Giulianotti, 2004). Several sports clubs had been set up by 1900 in emerging towns catering for competition in football and other sports. In the cities, football provides a personally pleasing leisure experience and a healthy social pastime, albeit also a temporary escape from the personal hazards of African city life. Bill Murray (1994) acknowledges that the practice of soccer is a cultural form in Africa, the most important aspect of which is the nature and practice of soccer fandom. He argues that soccer has always been regarded as the game of the people and attracts their participation, which ranges from moderate involvement to committed and animated identification.

Conceptual framing of online fan identities

Football has proven to be a fertile ground for the display and celebration of social identities. Studies (Giulianotti and Robertson, 2006; Burdsey and Chappell, 2002; Giulianotti, 1999; Gibson et al., 2002) have shown that supporting a football team goes beyond the 90 minutes on the pitch to affect all areas of a person's life. MacClancy (1996: 2) notes that 'sport in general and football in particular are vehicles of identity, providing people with a sense of difference and a way of classifying themselves and others, whether latitudinally or hierarchically.' Supporting a particular football team not only facilitates a feeling of shared identity with fellow supporters, it also acts as a means of differentiating oneself from other groups (Jenkins, 1996). In many cases identification with a particular team indicates what or who one is, and equally importantly, what or who they are not. Cyber fandoms also critically highlight that whilst supporters of a particular club may perceive themselves to be sharing a common identity, it is likely that in reality they will differ, both in terms of which aspects of 'the club' they identify with and their interpretation of what 'the club' represents.

A recent collection of work provides in-depth analysis of media and football identities in a European context. The collection edited by Roy Krøvel and Thore Roksvold (2012) entitled *We Love to Hate Each Other: Mediated Football Fan Culture* provides an interesting array of studies on fandom. For instance, Krøvel provides a discussion on how internet forums provide spaces to discuss critical issues such as football and ethnic identity among fans. With the relative anonymity and safety of the internet, people tend to speak more openly and are brazen about controversial issues such as ethnic tensions between fans. This is an interesting dimension within the Zimbabwean context, which is obvious when visiting sites belonging to Dynamos and Highlanders fans. Fans from both teams portray ethnic viewpoints using hurtful and hateful language. Cook and Hynes (2013) provide an important contribution to understanding how virtual spaces enable female fans to construct new and genderless personas while theorizing the political implications of the online selves they create. What is illuminating about this piece of work is how it resonates with experiences of a few female fans on the sites I targeted. As in Zimbabwe, Cook and Hynes show that although online spaces enable participants to create different and multiple identities, they are still gendered and enmeshed in dominant hegemonies. The language, nature of discussion, and the dominance of male views create spaces hegemonically masculinized to the extent that women are largely excluded.

The use of the Internet in social interactions allows people to express and articulate their identity (Marcus et al., 2006) through creating profiles on networks such as Facebook and Twitter (Siibak 2007). These spaces are providing people with a wide range of resources to define themselves. In discussing online fan identities, Baker (2009) posits two issues: first, fan identity occupies a middle area between 'real' and fantasy elements of self-presentation, and second, there is a mix of offline and online behaviors and attitudes among fans; thus the real and virtual combine. Such identities based on the real and virtual are what are known as blended identities; as Baker (2009: 13) notes, '"blended identity" refers to online self-presentations that include both online and offline aspects of themselves.' To understand the process of the creation of blended identity is to know how people: a) derive identities online related to their offline experiences and the online community they have joined; and then b) migrate from online to offline bringing with them online identities that they then introduce to others whom they have met first online. Football fans in Zimbabwe are in many ways occupying these blended identities.

Black (2006) argues that new information and communication technologies (ICTs) facilitate formation of 'virtual spaces' that cross-traditional cultural, linguistic, and geographic borders. In such 'virtual spaces,' personhood and relationality are being negotiated every day as people continuously create novel ways of interaction. Online spaces have in many ways emerged as new, transnational contexts for identity development. Fans use the internet as an extension of their identity, and although they may construct varying presentations of the self within cyberspace, this usually serves as a reinforcement of their idealized 'real life' identity (Kendall, 1998). Theorizing visual spaces has become an ever-important enterprise and people across the world are increasingly living in bifurcated spaces. Whilst updating web pages with messages, pictures, and chats is now an every-moment thing for many people, it now means they have a virtual and real self. This theorization can be best described by Goffman's dramaturgy in which people have a front and back stage. The virtual becomes the front stage where people spruce up their images and create selves that they best wish they were; yet the reality is the backstage. For football fandom, however, virtual spaces are not a bifurcation as such but simply an extension and platform to express already existing passions. The internet is just another means to outlay an intrinsic identity, thus, it is a virtual mirror that enhances the real and vice versa.

In this chapter, I also extend Bale's conceptualization of *placelessness*. Summarizing this concept, Bale (1998: 1) argues that it is 'the existence of relatively homogeneous and standardized landscapes which diminish the local specificity and variety of places that characterized pre-industrial societies. It is reflected in what is often felt to be a growing "sameness" in society.' When taken to analyze the impact of social media on football fandom, *placelessness* offers a critical view of how 'physical geography' as a distinct marker of fans has been contested and made obsolete. Advances in technology such as satellite television and the internet have allowed football teams, such as Manchester United of England, to defy geographical limitations and build online communities and global brands. The concept of *placelessness* aptly captures this phenomenon by highlighting how the ontological physicality of fandom can no longer be emphasized in defining fan communities. In Zimbabwe, such placelessness is more evident with online fan communities bringing together people all across the world of different sexes, ages, ethnicities, and even races. Following football matches, the latest news, debates and views, are all-available instantly across the world. Teams in many ways become symbols of space and place as fans link with each other globally and with those present in Zimbabwe. This connection with place is important in getting news, updates and gossip about the teams for those in the Diaspora (in the Zimbabwean case, this includes those in South Africa, United Kingdom, and Australia). This is an interesting dimension in that as the process of social networking makes football team *placeless*, it also instills a sense of place firmly in those who are far away from home.

To better illuminate fan 'communities' emerging online, I invoke Benedict Anderson's classic (1983) work on *Imagined Communities*. He argued that societies, in the process of forging new social identities, tend to emphasize a common community (somewhat artificially constructed) keen on state building (Gruzd et al., 2011). This concept of imagined communities, whilst used in a different setting, can be a useful starting point to discuss online fan communities in Zimbabwe. Anderson (1983: 6) argues that 'members of even the smallest nation will never know most of their fellow-members, meet them, or even hear of them, yet in the minds of each lives the image of their communion.' This is the same with fans on Facebook. They do not know each other and may never meet physically yet feels part of the same communion. Feelings of belonging are built on knowing and acknowledging the presence of other virtual residents. For example, Caps United fans on Facebook posting and debating various topics of interest have 'feelings of belonging' and a sense of community. To further explain this phenomenon, I employ Jones's (1997) notion of 'virtual settlement.' Jones (1997) argued that the prerequisite for an online community is the presence of a 'virtual settlement' that meets four conditions: interactivity; more than two communicators; a common public place where members can meet and interact; and sustained membership over time. Zimbabwean football fan groups on Facebook meet these four conditions and display highly organized 'virtual settlements.'

Firstly, posting, commenting on, and liking various topics, from historical artefacts to game-day performances and debates about best players, achieve interactivity. Interactivity is also gained by simply visiting the page frequently even without commenting. By reading and consuming what others are saying, fans build up a sense of belonging and relatedness to others on the site. This is what McMillan and Chavis (1986) call a sense of community (SoC). This sense of community is based on four dimensions in which people experience a sense of community if they feel: i) that they belong to the community (membership); ii) they can make a difference to the community (influence); iii) they provide support and are supported by other members (integration and fulfillment of needs); and iv) they share history, common places, time together, and similar experiences (shared emotional connection). Online football fans in Zimbabwe meet these four criteria and in many ways share a sense of community. As such, fan pages build up a sense of community amongst geographically spaced fans.

Organize in the virtual and meet in the real: Facebook and fan groups

Facebook has become an indispensable part of fan organization. It is now easier to meet a large number of fans in one place. Fans are becoming interconnected and share in their passion for football. Cellphone internet has made it easier for people to speak and share. For instance, fans are using Facebook to organize travel to away games. This phenomenon has developed sporadically over the years. At the turn of the century, Highlanders went on a run of winning four championships and through this period popularized fan travelling through what they call the *Bosso* Road Show. Recent years have seen an increase in fan travel and Facebooking has played a part in this. The walls of both Dynamos and Highlanders fan pages usually contain details about transport arrangements for those travelling to away games.

The negative aspect of this organizational ability of Facebook is that fans can now also plan to attack rival fans. Violence between fans is a recurring problem in Zimbabwe, especially in derby games that carry a lot of emotion; for example, Dynamos versus Highlanders games are often riddled with attacks amongst fans. Zimbabwean fans have historically rarely organized into fan clubs but are now able to plan and socialize with other fans whom they would never have related to without social media. Caps United fan platforms also engage in activities geared towards organizing match attendance. Towards game days the fan platforms are full of encouraging messages for people to attend matches. This is similar to other platforms where fans actively encourage others to show up at matches. With new relationships formed online there is increased peer pressure to attend matches. Most football fans have attended matches together for years without knowing each other beyond the stadium. In the era before cyberspace, meeting and networking with other fans in Zimbabwe was limited to the terraces. Many fans had no knowledge of other fans beyond their immediate circle of friends and family. Creation of online fan pages revolutionized fan relationships by offering spaces to meet people who share a similar passion. As an organizing tool, Facebook is slowly becoming an indispensable part of soccer fan networks in Zimbabwe.

Ethnicity and football identities

Often described by Robson Sharuko, editor of *The Herald* in Zimbabwe, as the 'Battle of Zimbabwe', matches between Highlanders and Dynamos are about dominance at national level; however, the rivalry goes deeper than football. For example, online sentiments by Dynamos fans show that they believe Highlanders fans hate them because they think Dynamos are related to ZANU PF, whom the Ndebele blame for the *Gukurahundi* massacres in the late 1980s. This refers to the suppression by Zimbabwe's Fifth Brigade in the predominantly Ndebele regions of Zimbabwe, most of which supported Joshua Nkomo. A few hundred disgruntled former

ZIPRA combatants waged armed banditry against civilians in Matabeleland, and destroyed government installations. The North-Korean-trained Fifth Brigade executed an estimated 20,000 civilians (For details, please see Catholic Commission for Justice and Peace (CCJP) and Legal Resources Foundation (LRF) (1997). The rivalry takes an ethnic, cultural, and political dimension. There is such a complex interplay of factors in choosing a team to support that it would be wrong to generalize all Highlanders fans as Ndebele and all Dynamos fans as Shona. There are many Shona people who support Highlanders, a team with a huge following in Harare, as can be seen when they play in the city. Dynamos also have a strong loyal base in Bulawayo, a city with high concentration of Ndebele. Though ethnicity plays an important part in football in Zimbabwe, it is not the only determining factor, as Chiweshe (2011) has shown that Dynamos fans are drawn from different ethnic groups and defy any singular ethnic definition. Social media have, however, offered new spaces for the interplay of ethnic rivalries. The celebration and derision of ethnic identities related to Zimbabwe's two biggest clubs provide insights into how football relates to ethnic identities. Facebook provides a platform for interplay of these processes and identities.

Sampled fan pages of the two teams were littered with messages either celebrating ethnic identities whilst deriding 'rival' ethnic identities; they eventually reached alarming levels. The language and description used to express dislike and hatred illustrated the fractured nature of ethnic identities in Zimbabwe. At the time of this research, Dynamos and Highlanders were involved in a tight championship race, which added to an already existing animosity. On Highlanders fan pages there were a lot of accusations of favoritism by the football authorities for Dynamos, especially following a decision to replay a game between Hwange and Dynamos due to violence against the coach. Within fan forums there are also debates and fights over ethnicity. Below is an extract from a thread on a Highlanders fan page highlighting how the team image has been created around an ethnic identity by some fans that believe that only Ndebele people are genuine fans.

Any fan that does not fit into this ethnic mold is regarded with suspicion. It is difficult therefore for most fans that belong to other ethnic groups to express their love for the team online without being abused.

Fan 1: *Wena . . . u r talking rubbish, the pioneer column first settled in Harare in 1890 b4 moving to Mat'land, thus, u were the first pple to b colonized so abathengisayo ngobani? Leza labelungu lizimpimpi zabo yini abahengisi bokugala* (Translation: What you are saying is utter nonsense. The pioneer column first settled in Harare in 1890 before moving to Matabeleland and hence Shonas were the first to be colonized. So who sold out? You came to Matabeleland with the whites and you were their sell outs and so you are the people who sold out)

Fan 2: *Shona from Zvimba and proud to support Bosso wholeheartedly since childhood.*

Fan 3: *Yes u r right there . . . Bosso z a futbol club for everyone that's y its called 'ithimu yezwe lonke' thats the identity of Bosso* (Yes you are right there . . . Bosso is a football club for everyone and that is why it is called 'The team for the whole nation')

Fan 4: *Bosso was formed by Lobengula's sons . . . So yiteam kaMthwakazi[2] u suckers!!!* (Bosso was formed by Lobengula's sons . . . So it's a Mthwakazian team)

Mthwakazi is the former name of the Ndebele kingdom that has now been resurrected by some Ndebeles seeking secession from Zimbabwe state.

Fan 5: *Hahaha, whoever is sayin tribalism does not exist in soccer is surely not human, aliboni abanye eItaly bekhalala ukudlala becoz of racism, these things are everywhere and itz happening, so deal with it coz iBosso ngeyesizwe sikaMthwakazi . . . Ngakho sharpa maNdebele, sharpa Bosso!!! 2013 s'yabangena . . . And hey, isizwe sikaMthwakazi involves everyone under Ndebele influence, abaseMatabeleland region, thatz y kulabeZansi, abeNhla, lamaHole* (Whoever is saying that tribalism does not exist in soccer is surely not human. Can you see that even in Italy there are some people who have refused to play football because of racism. Tribalism is everywhere and so you have to deal with the fact that Bosso is a Mthwakazian team. So big up to the Ndebeles, we are winning in 2013. The Mthwakazi nation involves everyone under the influence of the Ndebele).

On Dynamos fans' platforms, various fans posted the following sentiments, especially when rumors surfaced that Highlanders supporters had killed a Dynamos fan in Gweru:

Fan 1: *Bosso team yemandevere izere nemhondi* (Highlanders is a Ndebele team full of murderers)

Fan 2: *Vakapusa [Highlanders] sekuru wavo Lobengula vakatengesa nyika nekuda sugar* (Highlanders fans are as stupid as

---

[2] This is the former name of the Ndebele kingdom which has now been resurrected by some Ndebeles seeking secession from Zimbabwe state.

their great king Lobengula who sold land to white people for sugar)

Fan 3: We have suffered enough at the hands of these monsters. In Bulawayo we are always attacked yet we remain calm. Enough is enough this time it's war.

These sentiments provide a synopsis of the hatred, rooted in ethnicity that colors the Dynamos/Highlanders rivalry. In the era of social media, such hate speech gets amplified and spaces like Facebook provide platforms for interplay of these ethnic battles. Within the scope of this chapter it is impossible to directly quote thousands of ethnic based postings on fan platforms. In Zimbabwe, football thus cannot be separated from ethnic tensions.

The ethnic tensions are, however, not as strong when it comes to the rivalry between Caps United and Highlanders. It is through Facebook that we learnt of clashes between both sets of fans in a cup game between Caps United and Dynamos played at Barbourfields, the home of Highlanders in Bulawayo. The fans had joined forces against Dynamos but ended up fighting after Caps United was losing. Below are selected excerpts from Caps United and Highlanders fans commenting about the incident on different fan page:

Highlanders fan: They are all the same [Caps and Dynamos] you cannot trust a Shona.

Caps United: Violence pese pese, we did not ask them to come and support our team. It is not our fault that Highlanders went out early. Mandevere kungoda zvekurwa chete ndosaka vasina chinhu (Ndebele people love fighting that is why they are poor). Some of these sentiments are rarely aired in reality where ethnic tensions are subtler and understood differently. Social media platforms give the people liberty to freely air their sentiments without fear of a backlash.

What happens amongst football fans online or in stadiums is a microcosm of what pertains in everyday life. This is because football is such a popular and widely followed sport, especially amongst the poor majority in Zimbabwe. The sentiments and attitudes of football fans are, thus, a good indicator of general ethnic relations. Online posts by thousands of fans portray deep-rooted resentment between what are broadly defined as Ndebele and Shona.

Gender dimensions of online identities

Experiences of cyber fans in Zimbabwe show that online spaces are not disconnected from offline ideas of gender. Eklund (2011) noted that while these online arenas offer some space for redefinition of gender, users are at the same time constrained by their offline social context. The internet is a space where hegemonic masculinities are practiced and valorized. Whilst the anonymity of cyberspace has allowed women to navigate and occupy male spaces, the negative language and misogyny has followed online. What happens in cyberspace in many ways mirrors the behavior of the stadium. Fans use the same symbols that portray women as sexual objects and use the anonymity of the Internet to continue to spread misogynistic and homophobic sentiments.

On the Highlanders' page a fan posted a message about hatred for Dynamos by saying 'Dynamos is our [Highlanders] wife.' The meaning here is that women are weak and can easily be overpowered. A wife in the traditional sense is someone you paid *lobola* (bride price) for, thus she will do as you please at all times. This type of speech and language is characteristic of all male dominated pages. Below are other randomly selected statements from targeted fan pages that contained either misogynistic or homophobic statements:

Wakuita kunge hure manje, taura semurume (you are behaving like a prostitute, speak like a man)

Page rino rakazara vanhu vanofunga kunge vakadzi (this page is full of people who think like women)

Whilst the context of these statements is not provided here what is interesting are attitudes that men have towards women, who are seen as weak, unintelligent, promiscuous, sex objects, and inferior. However, fans also refer to football teams as second wives. As one fan noted on a post: *Kepe kepe [Caps United]mukadzi wechipiri* (Caps United is my second wife). This means that football teams are equated to a spousal level and are loved as such.

In this way, women are not necessarily demeaned but the fact that a man can love a team (which he sees once a week and has no ownership claim) in the same way he loves his wife is in itself problematic. Chiweshe (2007) has shown how Dynamos fans in Zimbabwe are in a committed relationship similar to marriage with the team. This relationship with the team is based on being part of larger community of fans, and social media has enhanced this connection. There are varied voices on Facebook advocating many things, but the pattern by and large remains patriarchal. This does not mean that all fans participate in or promote negative stereotypes about women. A few male online fans used social media platform to denounce the 2012 soccer star of the year, Denver Mukamba, for allegedly beating up his pregnant wife. One fan posted: '…a true gentleman does not beat up a woman, true gentlemen respect women…' Other comments, however, actually congratulated him for having multiple partners. What is clear is that fan pages remain highly masculinized spaces where women are often portrayed in negative ways.

Online fans as imagined communities

Three key issues arise when defining imagined communities. Firstly, Anderson (1983) argues that a key element of forming any type of community is the evolution of a common language. Online football fans have developed their own lexicon based on local lingos and those adopted from other areas. The language of the stadium has in many ways transferred to the cyberworld. An example is when Dynamos simply comment *zora* or *zora butter* (spread butter); this statement carries a lot of meaning for a person who belongs to this community. For an outsider spreading butter might have little significance or relation to football. *Zora butter* is a type of dance performed by Dynamos fans and players when they score or win. Additionally, Caps United fans regularly refer to each other as *Mukepe* (a play on the nickname of the team *Kepe kepe* which has no direct Shona equivalent or English translation). Gruzd et al. (2011) argue that the second issue to consider when discussing social media as imagined communities is temporality. For Anderson (1983), temporality has to do with the presence of the 'homogeneous time, in which a community is "moving" through history together by sharing a consciousness of a shared temporal dimension in which they co-exist' (Gruzd et al. 2011: 1303). Fans participating in online fan platforms in Zimbabwe appear to have a consciousness of a shared temporal dimension.

The third factor is what Anderson described as high centers in which societies are naturally organized around and under. At face value, Facebook poses as a decentralized system with a free flow of information, yet a closer look at fan pages outlines the existence of high centers. Cyber fans open Facebook accounts for a variety of reasons and do a lot more things on the site than just football. Club fan pages, however, have special importance and thus gain attention more than other things. This makes fan pages 'high centers' on Facebook, shaping online patterns and usage. One example that can highlight the importance of fan pages in the lives of fans is the outpouring of grief and condolences across fan platforms. The passing of Chicken Inn coach and Highlanders legend Adam Ndlovu in a car accident provides new understanding of how fans of football, despite their club affiliations, are part of a 'community', however it is defined or imagined. The spread of the news over Facebook with real time updates following the accident provides a telling example of how cyberspace can spread information across virtual football communities. Virtual football communities thus serve to reinforce both a group and an individual identity. Face-to-face meetings at stadiums are now augmented by online relationships that serve only to strengthen homogenous identities based on supporting a team.

Online fan identities as glocalized identities

Contrary to initial doom and gloom predictions – that the Western web would assimilate non-Western users in an act of cultural cannibalism –many online communities have, instead, co-opted online standards and adapted them to meet their needs, an effect known as 'glocalization.' Glocalization simply refers to the catchphrase 'think globally and act locally.' It is a combination of the words *globalization* and *localization*. Local communities or individuals take up global ideas, technologies, or artifacts and adapt them to their local conditions (Wellman, 2002). Africa's place in the increasingly interconnected web of nations, products, ideas, and practices is mediated in large part by its popular culture; and, in particular, its sporting culture. This unique sporting culture is a confluence of global and local practices that develops through introducing foreign practices into local conditions. Roudometof (2005) explains that the emerging reality of social life under the conditions of glocalization provides preconditions necessary for transnational social spaces, and that this process of glocalization may lead ultimately to a cosmopolitan society.

Social media offers an arena to understand how global fan practices, especially from leagues in European countries, have been exported to African contexts. Fans in Zimbabwe have picked up practices from other countries, creating a more transnational type of fan. From scarves, face paintings, flares, posters, *vuvuzelas* and other musical instruments, football have become a truly global game. Local practices and beliefs have been infused with these global practices. For example, paintings and messages on posters have local meanings and are in local languages. The phenomenon of social media or information technology was created in Western societies and transplanted to African contexts. As such, practices and uses of social media are dictated by the nature of the technologies involved. Being in front of a computer or on a cellphone does not negate localized knowledges and ways of doing things. One good example is the innovative language and ways of communicating that is now embraced by locals on social media.

Conclusion

The realm of the virtual is offering unlimited possibilities to our understanding of fan identities. This chapter has outlined how fans in Zimbabwe are increasingly engaged in cyber-fan identities that are an extension of their real-life fan identities. Football forms an integral part of a fan's life, including the virtual. Using ethnographic techniques, the discussion has nuanced interesting dimensions of cyber fandoms and virtual fan identities. It outlined how social media has extended spaces for fans to express and play out their fan identities. The chapter used various theoretical debates to provide a grounded understanding of online fan behaviors. Online fans are part of imagined communities based on supporting a common football team though networks formed in cyberspace. Social identity in the era of social media has become more complex as people are using the internet to portray, celebrate, and promote certain identities. Whilst the internet appears to be a democratic space where everyone is free to be what or who they want, this chapter has shown how class, gender, sexuality, and ethnicity still divide and organize people online. Social media also enhances the role of private individuals in spreading information as citizen journalists. Soccer fans online have been afforded the space to spread reports, rumors, and anecdotes. In conclusion, the chapter highlights how online identities are reflective and even an extension of everyday identities rather than of new identities.

Bibliography

Agnew, P. (2006) *Forza Italia: A Journey in Search of Italy and its Football*, London: Ebury Press.

Ahuvia, A.C. (2005) Beyond the Extended Self: Loved Objects and Consumers Identity Narratives. *Journal of Consumer Research* 32(1), 171–184.

Alber, E. and Ungruhe, C. (2016) Fans and states at work: a Ghanaian fan trip to the FIFA World Cup 2010 in South Africa, *Soccer and Society*, 17(1), 18-39

Alegi, P. (2010) *African Soccerscapes*. Ohio: Ohio University Press.

Alegi, P.C. (2002) Playing to the Gallery? Sport, Cultural Performance, and Social Identity in South Africa, 1920–1945. *The International Journal of African Historical Studies*, 35, 17–31.

Allon, F. (2000) Nostalgia Unbound: Illegibility and the Synthetic Excess of Place, *Continuum*, 14(3), 275-287

Armstrong, G. (1998) *Football Hooligans*. Oxford: Berg.

Armstrong, G. and Young, M. (2008) Fanatical Football Chants: Creating and Controlling the Carnival, *Sport in Society*, 2(3), 173-211

Amstrong, G. and Mitchell, JP. (2001) Players, Patrons and Politicians: Oppositional Cultures in Maltese Football. In G. Armstrong and R. Giulianotti (eds.) *Fear and Loathing in World Football*, Oxford: Berg

Armstrong, G. and Giulianotti, R. (2004) *Football in Africa*, New York: Palgrave Macmillan

Armstrong, G., and Giulianotti, R. (1997) *Entering the Field: New Perspectives on World Football*. Oxford: Berg.

Anderson, E. (2008) I Used to Think Women Were Weak:

Orthodox Masculinity, Gender Segregation, and Sport, *Sociological Forum* 23(2), 257-280

Anderson, E.M. 2007. *Women Watching Football: The Televisual Gaze and Female Spectatorship*. Master Thesis. Georgetown University.

Anderson, B. (1983) *Imagined Communities: Reflections on the Origin and Spread of Nationalism*, London: Verso.

Augé, M. (1995) *Non-places: Introduction to Anthropology of Supermodernity*, translated by John Howe. New York: Verso

Back, L. (2001) Sounds in the Crowd. In M. Bull and L. Back (eds) *The Auditory Studies Reader*, Oxford: Berg

Bairner, A. (2003) Political Unionism and Sporting Nationalism: An Examination of the Relationship Between Sport and National Identity Within the Ulster Unionist Tradition, *Identities: Global Studies in Culture and Power*, 10(4), 517-535

Bale, J., *Virtual Fandoms: Futurescapes of Football*, http://www.efdeportes.com/efd10/jbale.htm [Accessed 30 November 2012]

Baller, S. (2006) The Other Game: The Politics of Football in Africa, *Afrika Spectrum*, 41, 325–330.

Barker, A. (2009) Mick or Keith: Blended Identity of Online Rock Fans, *Identity in the Information Society (IDIS), Special Issue: "Social Identity on the web"* 2(1), 7-21

Ben-Porat, A. (2009) Not Just For Men: Israeli Women Who Fancy Football, *Soccer and Society* 10(6), 883–896.

Berger, A. (1986) Socialization. In *The Social World; An Introduction to Sociology*, eds. L. Tepperman and R.S. Richardson. London: McGraw-Hill.

Bhana, D. 2008. Six Packs and Big Muscles, and Stuff like that'. Primary School-aged South African Boys, Black and White, on Sport, *British Journal of Sociology of Education*, 29(1),

3–14

Black, R. (2006) Language, Culture, and Identity in Online Fan Fiction, *E–Learning*, 3(2), 170 – 184

Blumer, H. (1969) *Symbolic Interactionism: Perspective and Method*, Englewood Cliffs, NJ: Prentice-Hall.

Boyle, R., Giulianotti, R., and Williams, J. 1994. "We are Celtic supporters …" Questions of Football and Identity in Modern Scotland. In R. Giulianotti and J. Williams (eds.), *Game without Frontiers: Football, Identity and Modernity* (pp. 73–101), Aldershot: Arena.

Bradley, J.M. (2008) Celtic Football Club, Irish Ethnicity, and Scottish Society, *New Hibernia Review*, 12(1), 96–110

Burdsey, D., and Chappel, R. (2002) *'Soldiers, Sashes, Shamrocks: Football and Social Identity in Scotland and Northern Ireland'* http://physed.otago.ac.nz/sosol/v6i1/v6i1_1.html

Carter, D. (2005) Living in Virtual Communities. Ethnography of Human Relationships in Cyberspace, *Information, Communication & Society*, 8(2), 148-167.

Caudwell, J. (2002) Women's Experiences of Sexuality within Football Contexts: A Particular and Located Footballing Epistemology, *Football Issues*, 5(1), 24–43.

Caudwell, J. (1999) Women's Football in the United Kingdom: Theorising Gender and Unpacking the Butch Lesbian Image, *Journal of Sport and Social Issues*, 23(4), 390–402.

Chiweshe, M.K. (2016) Till death do us part: football as part of everyday life amongst Dynamos Football Club fans in Zimbabwe, *African Identities*, DOI: 10.1080/14725843.2015.1102703

Chiweshe, M.K. (2013) Online Football Fan Identities and Cyber-fandoms in Zimbabwe. In *Identity and Nation in African Football: Fans, Community and Clubs* (eds) C. Onwumechili, and G. Akindes (pp. 236–253). New York:

Palgrave Macmillan.

Chiweshe, M.K. (2012) *Of Goals and Whores. Football and Misogyny in Zimbabwe.* Paper presented at Rhodes University Critical Studies Seminar Series, Grahamstown, South Africa, August 17.

Chiweshe, M.K. 2011. Understanding the Processes of Becoming a Football Team Fan in an African Context: The Case of Dynamos Football Club Fans in Zimbabwe, *Soccer and Society*, 12 (), 174–183.

Clark, L.S. (1998) Dating on the Net: Teens and the Rise of 'Pure' Relationships. In *Cybersociety 2.0 Revisiting Computer-Mediated Communications and Community,* S.G Jones (ed.), pp. 159 – 183, Thousand Oaks: Sage.

Cochrain, V. (2005) *A Men's World. An Analysis of Italian Fan Survey.* www.gurdianfootball.com

Collinson, I. (2009) Singing Songs, Making Places, Creating Selves': Football Songs and Fan Identity at Sydney FC, *Transforming Cultures eJournal,* 4(1), 15-27

Connell, R.W. (2005) *Masculinities,* 2nd edition, Berkeley: University of California Press

Connell, R.W. (2000) *The Men and the Boys.* Berkeley: University of California Press.

Connell, R.W. (1987) *Gender and Power,* Stanford: Stanford University Press

Connell, R.W., and Messerschmidt, J.W. (2005) Hegemonic Masculinity: Rethinking the Concept, *Gender and Society* 19, 829–859.

Cooley, C. (1986) Socialization. In *The Social World; An Introduction to Sociology,* L. Tepperman and R.S. Richardson (eds.). London: McGraw-Hill.

Cook, A. and Hynes, D. (2013) *From the Terraces to the Television Screen: Gender, Sexuality and the Challenges of Online Fandom,* www.inter-disdplinary.net/research/wp-content/uploads/2013/03/Cook-Hynes-Fandom.pdf

Curi, M. (2008) Samba, Girls and Party: Who were the Brazilian Soccer Fans at a World Cup? An Ethnography of the 2006 World Cup in Germany, *Soccer and Society*, 9(1), 111–134.

Dalpian, R. P. C., V. S. Zylbersztejn, Z. Batistella, and C. Rossi. (2013) Fanatical Women and Soccer: An Exploratory Study, *Soccer and Society*.
doi: 10.1080/14660970.2013.828598.

Daimond, A. (2010) The Most Beautiful Game or the Most Gender Violent Sport? Exploring the Interface between Soccer, Gender and Violence in Zimbabwe. In *Gender, Sport and Development in Africa: Cross-Cultural Perspectives on Patterns of Representations and Marginalization*, J. Shehu (ed), pp. 1–11. Dakar: CODESRIA.

Darby, P. (2000) Football Colonial Doctrine and Indigenous Resistance: Mapping the Political Persona of FIFA's African Constituency. *Culture, Sport, Society* 3(1), 61–87.

Del Fresno, M. (2011) *Netnografía. Investigación, análisis e intervención social. Editorial UOC, 1ª edición*, Barcelona, España

Demetriou, D.Z. (2001) Connell's concept of hegemonic masculinity: A critique, *Theory and Society*, 30, 337–361

Doyle, P. (2008) Zimbabwe's Dynamos could be Football's biggest Winners this Season,
http://www.guardian.co.uk/sport/blog/2008/sep/26/africanchampionsleague

Duke, V. (1991) The Sociology of Football: A Research Agenda for the 1990s, *Sociological Review*, 39, 581–597.

Dunn, C. (2014) *Female Football Fans: Community, Identity and Sexism*, Basingstoke: Palgrave Macmillan.

Dunning, E. (1988) *Roots of Football Hooliganism*, London:

Routledge.

Eklund, L. (2011) Doing Gender in Cyberspace: The Performance of Gender by Female World of Warcraft Players, *Convergence: The International Journal of Research into New Media Technologies,* 17 (3): 323 – 342

Elder, C.D. and Cobb, R.W. (1983) *The Political Uses of Symbols,* New York: Longman.

Erhart, I. (2011) Ladies of Besiktas: A Dismantling of Male Hegemony at In.nü Stadium, *International Review for the Sociology of Sport,* 48(1), 83–98.

Firth, R. (1973) *Symbols, Public and Private,* London: Allen & Unwin.

Fridy, K. and Brobbey, V. (2009) Win the Match and Vote for Me: The Politicisation of Ghana's Accra Hearts of Oak Kumasi Asante Kotoko Football Clubs, *Journal of Modern African Studies,* 47(1), 19–39

Gibson. H., Willming, C. and A. Holdnak. (1999) "'We're Gators … Not Just Gator Fans": Serious Leisure and University of Florida Football', *Journal of Sports Behaviour* 22(2), 397–425.

Giddens, A. (1984) *The Constitution of Society,* Cambridge: Polity Press.

Giulianotti, R. (2005) The Sociability of sport: Scotland Football Supports as Interpreted through the Sociology of Georg Simmel, *International Review for the Sociology of Sport,* 40(3), 289-306

Giulianotti, R. (2004) Between Colonialism, Independence and Globalization: Football in Zimbabwe. In *Football in Africa: Conflict, Conciliation and Community,* R. Giulianotti & G. Armstrong (eds.), (pp. 80–102), London: Palgrave Macmillan.

Giulianotti, R. (1999) The South American Fan: Study on

Football Hooliganism in South America, *Journal of Sport and Leisure*, 20, 25–46.

Giulianotti, R., and Armstrong, G. (2004) Drama, Fields and Metaphors: An Introduction to Football in Africa. In *Football in Africa* G. Armstrong & R. Giulianotti (eds.), (pp. 1–23) New York, NY: Palgrave Macmillan.

Giulianotti, R., and Robertson, R. (2006) Glocalization, Globalization and Migration. The Case of Scottish Football Supporters in North America, *International Sociology*, 21(2), 171–98.

Goffman, E. (1958) *The Presentation of Self in Everyday Life*, Edinburgh: University of Edinburgh, Social Sciences Research Centre.

Grooves, A. (2011) *Molding and Moving Bodies in a Neoliberal World: African Football Labor Migrants in Egypt*. Unpublished Thesis Submitted to the Department of Sociology, Anthropology, Psychology, and Egyptology. University of Cairo.

Gruzd, A., Wellman, B. and Takhteyev, Y. (2011) Imagining Twitter as an Imagined Community, *American Behavioral Scientist*, 55(10), 1294– 1318.

Gosling, V. (2007) Girls Allowed? The Marginalisation of Female Sports Fans. In *Fandom: Identities and Communities in a Mediated World*, J. Gray, C. Sandvoss, and C.L. Harrington (eds), (pp. 250–260), New York: New York University Press.

Harms, H. (1982) Die soziale Zeitbombe ist noch längst nicht entschärft, zur möglichen Funktion des Sports bei der Integration der ausländischen Arbeitnehmer und ihrer Familien. *Olympische Jugend 12.*

Hargreaves, J.A. (2000) *Heroines of Sport*. London: Routledge.

Heide, W.S. (1978) Feminism for a Sporting Future. In *Women and Sport: From Myth to Reality* (ed.) C. Oglesby, (pp. 195–202), Philadelphia, PA: Lea & Febiger.

Herald (2011) *Remembering Reinhard Fabisch.* Available from: http://www.herald.co.zw/remembering-reinhard-fabisch/ (Accessed 26 June 2016).

Hesse-Lichtenberger, U. (2006) More than a game: Schalke'04 vs. Borussia Dortmund: Willykommen to Germany. Available from: *http://www.fourfourtwo.com/features/ugly-tear-ups-classic-one-upmanship-and-plastic-phalluses-why-dortmund-vs-schalke-germanys* (Accessed 14 May 2009)

Hughson, J. and Free, M. 2006. Paul Willis, Cultural Commodities and Collective Sport Fandom, *Sociology of Sport Journal,* 23(1), 72-85

Jenkins, R. (1996) *Social Identity,* London: Routledge.

Jones, K. (2008) Female Fandom: Identity, Sexism, and Men's Professional Football in England, *Sociology of Sport Journal,* 25(4), 516–537.

Jones, I. (1994) Mixing Qualitative and Quantitative Methods in Sport Fan Research, *The Qualitative Report 3,* Available from: http://www.nova.edu/ssss/QR/QR3-4/jones.html (Accessed 18 August 2006).

Jones, Q. 1997. Virtual Communities, Virtual Settlements and Cyber-archaeology. *Journal of Computer Mediated Communication,* 3(3), Available from: http://www.nova.edu/ssss/QR/QR3-4/jones.html (Accessed 3 June 2014).

Keim, M. (2003) *Nation-Building at Play – Sport as a tool for Social Integration in Post- apartheid South Africa.* Oxford: Meyer & Meyer Sport (UK). Ltd.

Kendall, L. (1998) Recontextualizing Cyberspace: Methodological Considerations for Online Research. *In: Doing Internet Research: Critical Issues and Methods for Examining the Net.* S. Jones (ed.) (pp. 57-74), London: Sage

Keyton, J. (2001) *Communication Research, Asking Questions, Finding Answers,* New York: McGraw Hill.

Kimmel, M. (2002) Masculinity as Homophobia: Fear, Shame, and Silence in the Construction of Gender identity. In *Women, Culture and Society: A Reader.* B. Balliet and P. McDaniel (eds.) (pp. 200–215), Dubuque, IA: Kendall/Hunt

Kozinets, R.V. (2006) Netnography 2.0. In *Handbook of Qualitative Research Methods in Marketing,* R.W. Belk, (ed.), (pp. 129-142), Cheltenham, UN and Northampton, MA: Edward Elgar Publishing.

Krøvel, R. and Roksvold, T. (2012) *We Love to Hate Each Other: Mediated Football Fan Culture,* Göteborg: Nordicom.

Last, A. (2004) Containment and Counter-Attach: A History of Eritrean Football. In *Football in Africa,* Gary Armstrong and Richard Giulianotti, (eds.), (pp. 27-40), New York: Palgrave Macmillan.

Ligion, N. (2007) *It's all About the Ball: How Football Tells a Story of Africa,* AFST 376: African Society

Lodge, D. (1990) *After Bakhtin: Essays on Fiction and Criticism,* London: Routledge

MacClancy, J. (1996) *Sport, Identity and Ethnicity.* Oxford: Berg.

MacClancy, J. (1996) Sport, Identity and Ethnicity. *In* J. MacClancy (ed.), (pp.1-20), *Sport, Identity and Ethnicity,* Oxford: Berg

Mackay, A. (1994) Heartbeat of the City: Influence of Soccer in Rome, Available from:
http://www.123HelpMe.com/view.asp?id=38106
(Accessed 3 July 2007).

Madzimbamuto, F.D. (2003) A Hospital Response to a Soccer Stadium Stampede in Zimbabwe, *Emergency Medicine Journal*

20(6), 556–559.

Maguire, J.A. (2011) Sport, Identity Politics, Gender and Globalization, *Sport in Society*, 14(7-8), 994-1009

Mangezvo, P.L. (2006) Football Hooliganism in Zimbabwe: An Overview. In *Sports, Juju and Human Development*, (ed.) C. Mararike, (pp. 65–76). Harare: Mond Books.

Marcus, B., Machilek, F. and Schütz, A. (2006) Personality in Cyberspace: Personal Web Sites as Media for Personality Expressions and Impressions, *Journal of Personality and Social Psychology*, 90(6), 1014–1031.

Mare, A. (2010) *Facebooking the Zimbabwean Crisis at the Click of a Button: Emerging Citizen Journalism or a Pass Time Activity?* Paper presented as Digital Natives Workshop, Johannesburg, South Africa.

Marsh, P. and Frosdick, A. (2005) *Football Hooliganism*, Oxford: Oxford University Press.

McMillan, D.W., and Chavis, D.M. (1986) Sense of Community: A Definition and Theory, *Journal of Community Psychology*, 14(1), 6–23.

Moreira, R.P. (2013) Marta Past Messi: (Re)definitions of Gender and Masculinity, Patriarchal Structures and Female Agency in International Soccer, *Soccer and Society*. doi: 10.1080/14660970.2013.828592.

Moyo, J. (2011) Ziscosteel investment spearheads Zimbabwe brain gain, *Mail & Guardian*, Aug 17

Mudapakati, Y. (2011) *Facebook Me: Exploratory Study on Social Networking amongst Women's University in Africa, Zimbabwe*, Unpublished thesis, Women's University in Africa.

Murray, B. (1994) *Football: A History of the World Game*, England: Scolar Press.

Mutungamiri, L. (1998) Dynamos Turns 35 Today. *Parade*, March 1998.

Mzaca, V. 2012. *Social Networking and the Future of Political Reporting in Zimbabwe and Beyond*, Available from: http://www.newstimeafrica.com/archives/22070 [Accessed 12 July 2012]

Ncube, L. (2014) The interface between football and ethnic identity discourses in Zimbabwe, *Critical African Studies*, 6(2-3), 192-210

Nkwi, W.G. (2014) Shifting Identity and National Football Squad: Indomitable Lions to Tamed Lambs. In, *Identity and Nation in African Football: Fans, Community and Clubs*, C. Onwumechili and G. Akindes (eds.) (pp. 155-164), New York: Palgrave Macmillan

Odhiambo C.J (2008) Circulation of Media Texts and Identity: Deconstruction of the Post-colony. In *Culture, Performance and Identity. Paths of Communication in Kenya*. Kimani Njogu (ed), (pp. 131-144), Nairobi: Twaweza Communications Limited.

Pannenborg, A. (2010) *Football in Africa: Observations about Political, Financial, Cultural and Religious Influences*, Amsterdam: NCDO Publication Series Sport & Development

Peden, A. (1972) *The Rhodesian Herald March*, 2 1972

Pfister, G., V. Lenneis, and S. Mintert. (2013) Female Fans of Men's Football – A Case study in Denmark. *Soccer and Society*. doi: 10.1080/14660970.2013.843923.

Pope, S., and Kirk, D. (2014) The Role of Physical Education and Other Formative Experiences of Three Generations of Female Football Fans, *Sport, Education and Society*, 19(2), 223–240.

Porat, B. (2010) Football Fandom: A Bounded Identification, *Soccer and Society*, 11(3), 277 – 290

Purcell, R. (2013) An Integrative Vernacular: Ellison, Dante and Social Cohesion in the post-Civil Rights Era, *ELH*, 80(3), 917-944

Prus, R. (1995) *Symbolic Interaction and Ethnographic Research: Intersubjectivity and the Study of Human Lived Experience*, New York: SUNY Press.

Raftopoulos, B., and Yoshikuni, T. (1999) *Sites of struggle: Essays in Zimbabwe's Urban History*, Harare: Weaver Press.

Ramonet, I. (1999) El fútbol es la guerra. In S. Segurola (ed.), *Fútbol y pasiones políticas* (pp. 131-138). Madrid: Debate.

Ranger, T.O. (2010) *Bulawayo Burning: The Social History of a Southern African City*, Harare: Weaver Press.

Roudometof, V. (2005) Transnationalism, Cosmopolitanism, and Glocalization. *Current Sociology*, 53(1), 113-135.

Rowe, D. (2003) Sport and the Repudiation of the Global, *International Review for the Sociology of Sport* 38(3), 281-294.

Rushworth, S. Through the Wind and Rain. Available from: http://student.bmj.com/issues/04/07/life/294.php (Accessed 15 October 2007).

Selmer, N. (2004) *Watching the Boys Play*. Frauen als Fußballfans. Kassel: Agon Sportverlag.

Selmer, N., and A. Sülzle. (2008) Tivoli-Tussen and Girls in Football Kits, *Esporte e Sociedade* 3(9), 1–19.

Sharuko, R. (2011). Dynamos and Zora Butter Phenomenon, *The Herald*, 18 November.

Skille, E. (2008) Biggest but Smallest: Female Football and the Case of Norway, *Soccer and Society* 9(4), 520–531.

Small, C. (1998) *Musicking: the Meaning of Performing & Listening*, Middleton, CT: Weslyean University Press.

Siibak, A. (2007) Casanova`s of the Virtual World. How Boys Present Themselves on Dating Websites. In M. Muukkonen & K. Sotkasiira (eds.), *Young People at the Crossroads: 5th International Conference on Youth Research in*

Karelia; Petrozavodsk, Republic of Karelia, Russian Federation; September 1–5, 2006 (pp. 83–91), Joensuu University: Joensuun yliopisto.

Sir Norman Chester Centre For Football Research, (2002) *Fact Sheet 3, Why Support Football?* Leicester: University of Leicester.

Social Issues Research Centre, (2008) *Football Passions: Report of research conducted by The Social Issues Research Centre*, Commissioned by Canon

Spender, D. (1995) *Nattering on the Net: Women, Power and Cyberspace*, Melbourne: Spinifex Press.

Stuart, O. (1996) Players, Workers, Protestors: Social Change and Soccer in Colonial Zimbabwe. In J. MacClancy (Ed.), *Sport, Identity and Ethnicity* (pp. 167–180). Oxford: Berg.

Tajfel, H. (1972) La Catégorisation Sociale (social categorization), *Introduction à la psy-chologie sociale*, 1, 272–302.

The Society for More Creative Speech, (1996) *Symbolic Interactionism as Defined by Herbert Blumer*, Available from: http://www.thepoint.net/~usul/text/blumer.html (Accessed 3 June 2012).

Toffoletti, K., and P. Mewett. (2012) *Sport and its Female Fans*, New York: Routledge

Tunon, J. And Brey, E. (2012) Sports and Politics in Spain – Football and Nationalist Attitudes within the Basque Country and Catalonia, *European Journal for Sport and Society*, 9(1+2), 7-32

Uhler, B. and Murrell, A. (1999) Examining Fan Reactions to Game Outcomes: A Longitudinal Study of Social Identity, *Journal of Sport Behaviour*, 22(1), 15–37.

Wann, D.L., Melnick, M.J., Russell, G.W., & Pease, D.G. (2001) *Sport fans: The psychology and social impact of spectators*,

London: Routledge.

Wann, D., Royalty, J. and Roberts, A. (2000) The Self-Presentation of Sport Fans: Investigating the Importance of Team Identification and Self-Esteem, *Journal of Sport Behavior,* 23(2), 198–206.

Wann, D., Tucker, K. and Schrader, M. (2000) An Exploratory Examination of the Factors Influencing the Origination, Continuation and Cessation of Identification with Sports Teams, *Perceptual and Motor Skills* 82, 995–1001.

Wellman, B. (2002) Little Boxes, Glocalisation, and Networked Individualism. In *Digital Cities II* M. Tanabe, P. van den Besselaar, and T. Ishida (eds). Berlin: Springer-Verlag.

West, M.O. (2002) *The Rise of an African Middle Class in Colonial Zimbabwe 1898–1965,* Bloomington: Indiana University Press.

Williamson, M. (2005) *The Lure of the Vampire,* London: Wallflower Press

Zenenga, P. (2012) Visualizing Politics in an African Sport: Political and Cultural Constructions in Zimbabwean Soccer, *Soccer and Society,* 13(2), 250–263.

Zenenga, P. (2011) Aesthetics and Performance in Zimbabwean Soccer, *African Identities,* 9(3), 323–336.

Printed in the United States
By Bookmasters